THE "NEW PICK" CARS.

PRICE 170 GUINEAS.   14-16 H.P.   4 Cylinders.

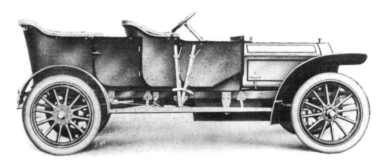

PRICE 195 GUINEAS.   14-16 H.P.   4 Cylinders.

MAKERS—

The "New Pick" Motor Co.,
STAMFORD.

Plate 1: Advertisement for the "New Pick" cars
from Dolby's *Directory of Stamford and Rutland* (1910)

PICK OF STAMFORD

A history of the Pick Motor Company

Michael Key

PAUL WATKINS

STAMFORD

Published by

PAUL WATKINS
18, Adelaide Street
Stamford, Lincolnshire
PE9 2EN

ISBN

1 871615 53 4

Frontispiece and title-page illustrations:
2. Photograph of John Henry Pick (1867-1954)
from W. T. Pike's *Stamford with Oakham and
Uppingham Temp. George V* (Brighton, 1911)
3. Advertisement for the 'Special Doctor's Coupé'
from the 1912 Catalogue of the Pick Motor Company

Printed and bound by Woolnough Bookbinding, Irthlingborough

CONTENTS

ACKNOWLEDGMENTS

There are many people and institutions to thank for their help through conversations and letters and in loaning material during the research into one of the forgotten motor car makers. Firstly, there is my old friend Chris Davis who generously passed over his notes on the firm, it having been his intention to write the history. So, I suppose, this book should have been written by him. Then there are the present owners of surviving Pick cars — Shauna Lord, Reg Long, Clem Maclachan and Len Everitt — who have patiently responded to my questions. Almost a whole book would be needed to list everyone who has helped. Many are mentioned in the text or on the captions to illustrations; I hope those who are not will forgive me, but to all of you I extend my grateful thanks.

Researching obscure and forgotten firms such as the Pick Motor Company is rather like being on a safari through an uncharted land: one always comes across the unexpected. Bicycles might be anticipated as part of the background to motor manufacture, but not garden tools and rug needles! Another surprise is the small number of surviving Pick cars. However, there is one mystery that has not been cleared up satisfactorily: that of the Pick motor cycle. One such was unearthed a few years ago and has been restored. It now lives in Gloucestershire. Michael Worthington-Williams described and illustrated it in *Classic Motor Cycle* in May 1991. The machine carries a Leicestershire licence plate and when found had a tax disc showing the name 'Pick'. The engine is a Dalm of 5/6 h.p. On the petrol tank it has a transfer of the Leicester Cycle Company. Now, there is no evidence that Pick of Stamford ever made a motor cycle. 'Jack' Pick, in his memoirs, makes no mention of one. W. H. Edinborough, who worked for Pick, did make up a motor cycle using a De Dion engine and a second hand frame but it was an isolated creation for his own use. It seems unlikely that Pick would have given his blessing to such a project; but where did the mystery machine originate? My suggestion is that it came from Henry Pick who was a bicycle maker in St. Mark's Street, Leicester, between about 1900 and 1927, but I shall leave someone else to explore that path.

Michael Key

Plate 4, overleaf: Photograph of 1901 or 1902 Pick Voiturette, Reg. No. C 584
Stamford Museum, original loaned by T. Harding

Plate 5, opposite: The 1914 four-seater standing in Barnack Road near
to the company's works, *Stamford Museum, original loaned by L. Carnall*

PICK OF STAMFORD

Before the First World War the British motor industry (with some notable exceptions such as Ford, Wolseley and Humber) was akin to a cottage industry. All over the country former bicycle makers, blacksmiths, even a few real engineers, set up small workshops to express their individual, often eccentric, ideas of what a motor car should be. Only half of the two hundred or so makes launched at this time survived the war and many of these did not continue beyond 1925. Even fewer became today's household names, most being remembered only by the enthusiast. One such is the Pick, built in the small country market town of Stamford, Lincolnshire. An improbable centre for motor manufacturing perhaps, but one whose products were to find their way to the furthest corners of the world.

John Henry Pick was born in the Welland Cottage Inn, 11 Gas Street, an area of poor, working-class, terraced housing in Stamford, on 22 October 1867. 'Jack', as he was usually called, and his brother Walter, were sons of Robert Pick, a butcher and publican, and his wife Catherine. His education appears to have been rudimentary, and after attending St Michael's and St Martin's schools he began work at Thomas Turner's brickworks in Casterton Road when he was thirteen. He did not stay long, saying later that he did not relish the thought of losing a finger in the brick press as did many of the lads there. His next step was a short stint as errand boy for Edward Young, a grocer in St John's Street. While there he worked out a quick and easy way to cut lump sugar cones and sieve the result into caster and granulated grades. This time saving operation illustrates the mechanical aptitude that was to lift him from the ranks of the ordinary worker to become a manufacturer and employer in his own right.[1]

At the age of sixteen Jack left home to be apprenticed to a blacksmith named Birchnall at Little Bytham, ten miles north of Stamford. With Birchnall he learned not only the art of shoeing but also basic engineering skills, repairing farm tools and implements. He was a good pupil and he soon found himself sent to the nearby Rutland village of Clipsham to join Birchnall's journeyman there. While at Clipsham he developed his lifetime's love of cricket, football and country sports, pursuits which sometimes got in the way of other more important activities. The manner of his leaving Clipsham illustrates this well. Within a few days of finishing his apprenticeship he was late returning from cub hunting and failed to do a promised shoeing job and was sacked. However, not all his spare time was given over to sport; Clipsham was where he met his future wife, Emily Brewster.

Having lost his job young Jack Pick left the village and headed for Staffordshire where he found a place in a shoeing shop at Stone. He stayed for only a few months and in 1887 returned to Stamford to find a job in the blacksmith's shop at George Jeffery and Edward Blackstone's engineering works. His training with Birchnall must have been thorough for within eighteen months he had risen from the lowest single-handed fire to become foreman blacksmith. The resulting increase in wages enabled him to marry Emily in Clipsham church.

During his time at Clipsham, Pick had met John Harrison who later, in about 1890, set up the Harrison Patents Company to promote and exploit new ideas for agricultural implements and in general engineering. The site of his works in Wharf Road, Stamford, had successively been a foundry, a paper mill and a terra cotta works and is now (1994) the premises of steel stockholders and general ironmongers McArthur Gray Ltd. Pick said he worked at Harrison's for a time and it was while there that he made, in partnership with Thomas Roy Fountain, an iron merchant's manager, his first successful patent application. This was for an improved weed hoe. It had a flat blade with two cutting edges set forward at an angle relative to the handle so that when in use it lay horizontal. It was used in a pushing and pulling action (see plate 6).[2]

In 1894 Pick had another patent published, this time in partnership with Henry Thomas Daniels, an iron merchant of Horseshoe Lane, Stamford. This patent related to improving the adjustable sockets and shanks for garden implements. The socket or shank of the handle and the tool tang were each flattened at the end with a serrated surface through which a bolt and nut drew them together. The serrations allowed the angle of the tool in relation to the handle to be altered.[3]

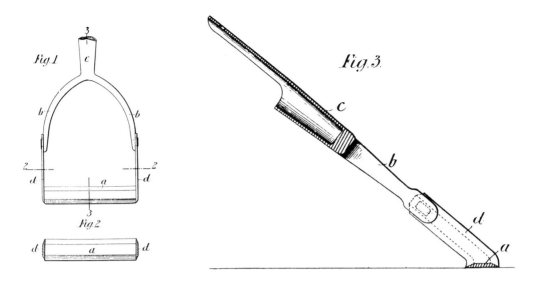

Plate 6: Pick's first patent, the 1893 'Improvements in and relating to Hoe Blades'
(Patent 8044, 1893), from the published specifications

Pick claimed to have been recalled to Blackstone's at about this time to help solve problems with an order for a rotary digger from Messrs Briggs and Holland, a firm of steam cultivating contractors at Priory Farm, Stamford. The machine apparently worked well enough on dry ground but was prone to clogging on wet. What Pick did to resolve the problem, if in fact he ever did, is not recorded but it was something he had to turn his attention to again some years later.[4] Soon after this, in about 1895, Pick decided to set up on his own account and took a shop on the corner of St Leonard's Street and Brazenose Lane. Here with a home-made wooden lathe and financial help from Cecil Fountain, who later became manager to Charles Gray, another Stamford ironfounder, he produced his patent hoes. These were available in six different sizes from 3½ in. to 8 in. wide at prices from 1s. 6d. to 2s. 6d. each. Another product of this period was a rugging needle which Pick claimed to have patented, a claim which research in the Patent Office has failed to confirm.

The following year, 1896, saw a dramatic boom in bicycle production, and Pick, just like many another small town entrepreneur, saw an opportunity to exploit the demand for bicycles. In May Pick went into partnership with Anthony John Pledger, a local ironmerchant, as cycle dealers and fitters. With Pledger providing the finance, Pick moved to new premises at 5 Blackfriars Street. This agreement, which was for only six months (none of Pick's partnerships seem to have lasted very long), enabled him to lay the foundation for his later business enterprises.[5] Under the title 'J. H. Pick and Co', with two employees (his brother Walter and an un-named former Blackstone's machine shop foreman), he set to work repairing and selling cycles, doing light engineering jobs and making his hoes and needles, the latter selling for sixpence halfpenny each.

This was also the year that H. J. Lawson founded the British Daimler company and the year that Frederick Lanchester and Herbert Austin built experimental motor cars. It was also the year, in November, that the Locomotive Acts of 1865 and 1878 were repealed, to be replaced by the Locomotives on Highways Act which permitted motor cars to travel freely on the roads at a speed not exceeding 12 m.p.h. In celebration of this last event the first London to Brighton 'Emancipation' run took place on the 14th of November. The acceleration of technical development which followed transformed the horseless carriage into a recognisable motor car within ten years. What Pick knew of these events is unknown, but he would certainly have heard about, indeed may have seen, what was probably the first motor car to pass through Stamford. Late one August evening in 1897 two men travelling from London to Newcastle on Tyne had the misfortune to damage their car 'while they were dodging a runaway horse'. After spending the night in the town while the car was repaired they continued on their journey the next day. What a pity the local newspaper did not record the names of these pioneers.[6]

The boom which had brought Pick into the bicycle trade collapsed in 1897 as a result of the importation of cheap mass-produced American machines and the over production by a number of English profiteering enterprises set up by H. J. Lawson. However, the bicycle was now not merely a form of recreation for the well to do, but had become an essential form of transport for the working man. Because of this trend Pick was able to survive and even to prosper and his company's work force grew to twelve. Pick introduced several new ideas to his bicycles, such as a self-contained cycle stand and a brake which acted on the wheel rim instead of on the upper surface of the tyre (the more usual method). His applications in 1898 to patent both were not accepted but the following description of the brake was published in the *Stamford Mercury*.

> Messrs Pick and Co, cycle makers, Stamford, have just taken out a patent for a new bicycle brake upon an entirely new principle. The invention is an ingenious one, and there can be no doubt as to its utility. The brake is fixed on the front fork of the machine, the same as the foot rest. Underneath the rest is a tube, around which there is a spring, inside the tube is a piece of rubber. When the brake has to be applied, the rider must place his feet in the rest and lower his heels, and by a clever contrivance the rubber shoots out and binds the rim on each side of the fore wheel. The brake is fixed so that the speed can easily be regulated, and in its use there is no fear of damaging the tyre. It really forms a double brake, one on each side of the fore wheel, and they act independently of each other. If one side happens to fail, the leverage on the other side can be applied with the desired effect. It is a compact piece of work, and has the advantage of being considerably less in weight than the hand brakes in general use at the present time. [7]

This report has the hallmark of the official press release about it. In his advertising Pick chose the slogan 'Pick of All', avoiding the more obvious and hackneyed line 'Pick of the Bunch'. By 1899 he was able to advertise '150 ....

10

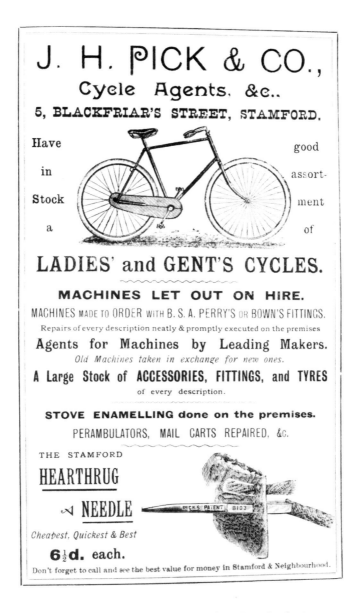

Plate 7: Advertisement for J. H. Pick & Co., Cycle Agents.

Cycles, differing in design and detail, but everyone guaranteed equal in construction.' Now, with a work force said to be around forty, cycles could be built to special order within four days and prices were claimed to be below any other leading maker.[8] With a work force of such a size conditions at 5 Blackfriars Street had become extremely cramped so the adjacent premises were acquired.

In March 1899 Pick organised a two day Cycle Show in the Stamford Assembly Rooms. Over a hundred bicycles 'with the latest improvements' were

Plate 8: The "Pick of All" Model A cycle, from the company's catalogue of *c.*1900
Phillips Collection, Stamford Town Hall

on show and a local draper's, Oates and Musson, had a large array of cycle costumes on display. Among the items which greatly interested those who visited the show were a voiturette and a motor cycle exhibited by The Motor Manufacturing Co. of London. How they came to be included is not known. As organiser or promoter of the show Pick must have invited the company, and this can be seen as evidence of his interest in cars at this time. It may well have been this car (which Pick described later as a Panhard) and the memory of those visiting motorists two years earlier which fuelled his ambition to build his first car. Having obtained an engine 'of French design', possibly a De Dion, he began to experiment, and installed it in a dog-cart style body.[9]

Pick later recalled that he sold the first result of his work to a Dr Benson of nearby Market Deeping for £85. A second car was bought by the Marquis of Exeter. These cars were fully road tested before sale. In June 1900 Pick drove to Barnet, near London, a distance of about seventy miles in approximately five hours. The journey was uneventful until, at Stilton on the return, an exhaust valve broke. A telegram was sent to Stamford for a replacement and the trip was successfully completed the next day. On a journey to Oxford in August, Pick and a companion were in collision with a butcher's cart near Northampton. There were no casualties, although the car did sustain some damage to the woodwork. Accidents of this kind were not rare. In an early outing with his first car, Pick, with the famed Frank and Evershed Carter of Blackstone and Company as passengers, set out late one evening to go to Edith Weston, to the west of Stamford. This was a round trip of about eight miles. With only two candle lamps

12

Plate 9: Jack Pick road-testing the two-seater on Priory Road, Stamford, in 1900.
The car is fitted with his patented front suspension and tiller steering
Stamford Museum, original photograph loaned by P. Cross

they blundered along at about ten miles an hour, 'the lights were quite good, they could see at least two feet ahead', and ran off the road and crashed through a closed gate! Somewhat chastened they gave up and returned more sedately to Stamford to try again the next morning, in daylight.[10]

It is interesting to note that the *Stamford Mercury* found these events newsworthy enough to report, considering that during the same year they failed to record that Herbert Austin drove the first prototype Wolseley in a 1,000 miles reliability trial to win a silver medal. A watershed event. 'It is no exaggeration to say that this trial first set the wheels of the British motor industry in motion, albeit slow motion.'[11]

Later that same year, 1900, J. H. Pick and Co. exhibited at the Stanley Cycle Show held in the Agricultural Halls, Islington, London. Along with his bicycles Pick sent two cars. In many respects the two cars were alike. The first was a dog cart with a 4¼ h.p. single cylinder De Dion vertical water cooled engine geared directly to the rear axle through two friction clutches. A change speed lever for the two gears was placed between the front seats. The frame was of tubular construction with cycle type road wheels. The front wheels were carried in tubular forks similar to those on a bicycle and joined at the head. They were joined to the chassis frame by curved leaf springs, which allowed the wheels a certain amount of independent vertical movement. This spring system, for which

13

Plate 10: Illustration of the Pick Voiturette in *The Automotor Journal* (December, 1900).
A similar illustration appears in *The Motor-Car Journal* (November 24th, 1900, p. 635)

Pick had made a successful patent application earlier in the year, was an attempt
to remove the unpleasant jolting experienced when driving over the rough roads
of the day. The three or four seater body was finished in crimson with black and
white lining.

    The second car was a voiturette driven by a vertical air-cooled 2¾ h.p.
engine. The cooling air was gathered by a funnel shaped scoop under the front
of the car and directed onto the single cylinder. Both cars were fitted with
surface carburettors. As in the dog cart the transmission was through two friction
clutches on a shaft from the side of the motor case. Two small gears, one with 16
teeth, the other with 32 teeth, attached to the friction clutches meshed with two
larger gears, 124 and 132 teeth respectively, on the driving axle. The clutches
were operated by a single change speed lever. Moving the lever to the right
engaged the slow speed gear, to the left the high speed gear. Speeds of ten and
twenty five miles an hour were claimed. The gears were enclosed within a casing
which also housed a foot operated band brake. A hand brake, which looked like
a large spoon, acting on the rear tyres, was operated from the driver's seat. This
car was painted green lined out with black and white.[12]

    On his return to Stamford Pick was approached by a group, which consisted
mainly of local gentry, with the idea of forming a company to produce Pick's
cars. On 19th March 1900 the Pick Motor Company Ltd was launched with a
capital investment of £10,000 'to carry on the business of bicycle and motor car
manufacturers previously carried on by J. H. Pick and C. Gray'. The board of

14

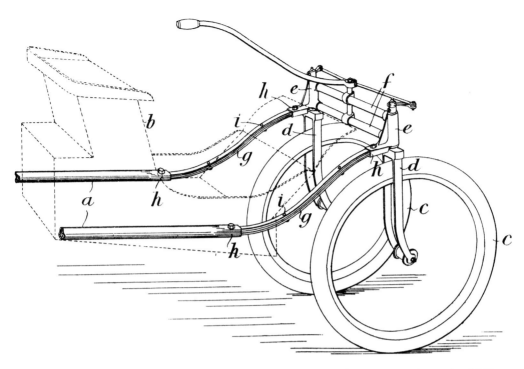

Plate 11: Illustration of the front suspension system of the same car from the 1900
patent no. 12,610 'Improvements in self-propelled road vehicles'
from the published patent

directors were the Marquess of Exeter (chairman); Sir George Whitcote, Bart; W.
Bean Esq. of Wothorpe, and Charles Gray Esq. They were later 'joined by Rev. Mr
Tryon, minister of the Baptist church. The latter's interest was aroused by his son
Henry Tryon, who, as a lad of 18, was an enthusiastic mechanic.' Mr Tryon was
later described by Jack Pick as having

> a nice line in salesmanship, whenever a prospective purchaser hovered on
> the horizon he [would] dwell on the beauties of the car. The Reverend
> gentleman would place a marble on the wing of the vehicle before starting
> his journey [and state that] it would be in the same position on his return
> home . . . not one of the customers ever expressed a doubt as to the veracity
> of this claim.[13]

Most of the tools and equipment already in Pick's works were suitable for
the manufacture of motor cars; after all they were little more than motorised
bicycles. There was probably some new plant to be acquired but no record of this
survives. Later, engine and gearbox castings were to come from Charles Gray's
iron foundry on St Mary's Hill but for now De Dion engines were used.

When the firm which bore his name was founded, Jack Pick was not
appointed a director; he became works manager with no say in the running of
the business. There is no doubt that this decision led to many of the problems
later faced by the new firm. There were continual disagreements between him

15

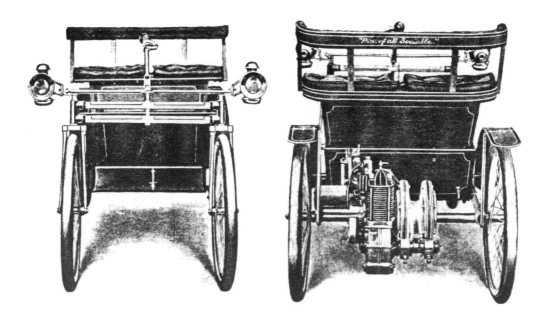

Plate 12: Front and rear views of the car from *The Autocar* (Dec. 1st, 1900, p. 1179). Similar views appeared in *The Motor-Car Journal* (Nov. 24th, 1900, p. 635)

and the board of directors. Pick, whose outspoken and down to earth language undoubtedly provoked the directors, seems to have been constantly exasperated with the board. Apart from Charles Gray he was the only one with any engineering background, but he was often overruled on decisions of a mechanical nature. He also had no say in trading policy. The selling off at discounted prices of the entire stock of cycles and the disposal of the cycle building plant in March 1902 was a typical cause of conflict. Many years later Pick was still bitter about the decision: 'a perfectly sound business, that of cycle manufacture, was not kept up but the plant dismantled. From the start therefore, there was no income only expenditure in the replacement of machines suitable for car building. At a later date when the firm got into difficulties a flourishing cycle making branch would have well proved its worth.'[14] Be that as it may, it does seem to have been a grave error of judgement to abandon a known and reliable source of income in favour of what was still, despite its success, a speculative product. Another disagreement between Pick and the board was over the type of engine for the new models in 1902. Pick favoured the vertical type used successfully so far, the board wanted a completely new horizontal type.

The cars the new company displayed at the 1901 Automobile Club exhibition, held again at Islington, were similar to the previous year's offerings.

16

The main difference was the uprating of the engines: the voiturette was now 3½ h.p., while the dog cart was now fitted with a two cylinder 6 h.p. water cooled engine.[15] Pick's patent, No. 12,610. 1901, for the leaf spring system of connecting the front wheels to the main chassis had now been accepted and published. For the 1902 Crystal Palace Motor Show the Pick Motor Co. put on a most eye-catching presentation with five cars all painted white with gold lining.[16] Two were the little voiturettes with the single cylinder, water cooled 4 h.p. engine as shown at the previous year's Automobile Club exhibition. Alongside were three new models; a two cylinder voiturette with a 6 h.p. engine, a tonneau and another voiturette with two cylinder 10 h.p. engines. All three of these new cars had horizontally opposed water cooled engines mounted transversely at the front end of the chassis forward of the dashboard under the bonnet. They were designed and made by the firm. The board had once again got its way.

> The new engines excited a good deal of attention – by having the connecting rods in the centre of the piston, but the pistons slightly out of line. The cylinders are so arranged that they retreat from and approach the crank shaft at the same time. This tends to produce a vacuum in the air-tight rectangular crank chamber, in which splash lubrication of the free ends of the pistons is effected, and at the same time any tendency of the lubricating oil to get into the explosion chambers of the cylinders is effectively prevented. The half speed gear for exhaust and ignition is mounted, as will be seen, on the top of the crank chamber. The method of transmission is as unconventional, if not as original as the engine. Two cross belts from different sized pulleys on the crank drive on to loose and fixed pulleys on a countershaft behind the rear axle.[17]

A sliding clutch between the two pulleys, one high speed, the other low speed, on the counter shaft engaged a sprocket from which a chain was connected to the differential on the live rear axle. The radiator was set in front of the engine with the water tank under the front seat and the fuel tank was behind the dashboard. A major change was the fitting of a steering wheel on a raked steering column. Prices were £130 for the 4 h.p. model and £150 for the 6 h.p.[18]

Pick cars were 'chiefly remarkable for their low prices' but 'the wisdom of fitting a 10 h.p. motor to a belt transmission remains to be seen'. So wrote one motoring correspondent. Later in the year a flurry of letters in the *Autocar* came to the conclusion that the lowness of the prices was attributable to the use of belt drive and that it had no adverse effect on performance. Among belt drive's advantages were its flexibility and its noiselessness. One of the car's champions was H. T. Benson, J.P., L.R.C.P., who wrote that he had driven his 6 h.p. voiturette for over six thousand miles and had no trouble with the belts. H. T. Benson was the Market Deeping doctor to whom Pick had sold his very first car. Benson, who died in 1942 aged 83, was one of the first in south Lincolnshire to own a motor car.

Another satisfied correspondent was F. Carter. He wrote that he had recently driven his 10 h.p. tonneau with 'four up, to Sussex and back, a distance of over four hundred miles'. Despite the dirty roads and having to cross an eighteen inch deep ford the journey was completed without a hitch. Carter stated that 'for finish, comfort in riding, reliability, and ease of management — I do not know of another car of the same horse power within £100'.[19] The author was doubtless Frank Carter, one of the Carter brothers whose oil engines formed the basis for Messrs Blackstone's successful transition from steam. The Carters, who originated from Billingshurst in Sussex, moved to Stamford in 1896. Frank and Evershed were early supporters of Pick and had themselves experimented with an early motor car. No description survives other than that it ran on 'iron tyred wheels like one would have seen on a cart'.[20] A tradition in the Carter family has it that Pick learned all he knew from the brothers. There may well be an element of truth in this assertion. He, like them, had worked for Blackstone and obviously knew them well enough to take them out in his first car. They must have discussed engines and related subjects (what else would engineers talk about?) and some of the Carters' knowledge and experience must have rubbed off. Indeed, it may be asked, where else would Pick have gained the knowledge to produce a viable and reliable motor car so quickly?

For the 1903 Crystal Palace Motor Show the Pick Motor Co. displayed eight variously bodied cars based on the previous year's models. Despite good reports on the use of their belt drive the company did make improvements to the casing, giving better protection from wet and dirt. They also added to the range two chain driven cars, a 6 h.p. and a 10 h.p., each using the now standard horizontally opposed engine. Transmission was from a clutch shaft, which was an extension of the engine crankshaft, to a gearbox by a Renold chain. The gearbox was of the Panhard type with three forward and one reverse gears with a chain drive to the rear axle. The change speed lever was mounted beside the steering column. Similar gearboxes were fitted to the belt driven models. Pick's patented cam brakes which acted on the rear wheel hubs were fitted as standard.

> The brake to be found on the cars made by the Pick Motor Company Limited, is novel, because, despite its absolute simplicity, it is of wonderful power. We give a view of the brake, and a sketch showing the boxes and the cam which operates the brake. The boxes are attached to the ends of the leather-lined metal band, and when the cam has its major axis upright the band is loose on the drum; when the brake shaft is partly revolved in either direction, the cam moves the boxes in opposite directions and towards each other, thereby tightening the band on the drum. The grip is wonderful, and we were able with one finger to oppose any efforts of others to revolve the wheel, it is simple but thoroughly effective.[21]

One wonders why, if Pick's cam brake was such a simple and powerful improvement on the braking systems of the day, he did not further its development. Possibly another case of directorial interference.

18

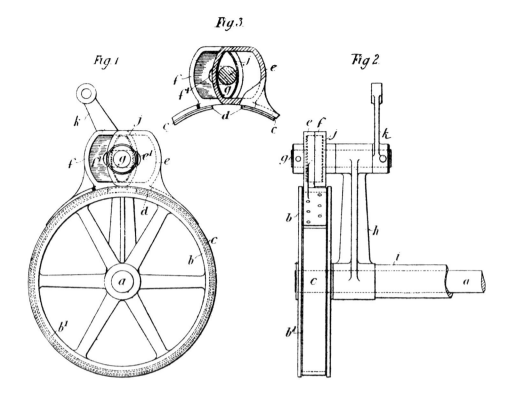

Plate 13: The specification for Pick's improved braking mechanism,
from the published patent (no. 26,685, dated Dec. 3, 1902)

Plate 14: Illustrations of the 1902 Pick 10 h.p. voiturette engine, from *The Automotor
Journal* (March, 1902, p. 231)

Plate 15: Crystal Palace Motor Show, 1903, a general view of the exhibits, looking towards the North. Photograph from *The Car*, issue no. 37 (February 4, 1903), p. 371

20

Plate 16: Crystal Palace Motor Show, 1903, a view of the centre transept, from *The Car*, issue no. 37 (February 4, 1903), p. 370

21

The
"PICK" CARS
are BRITISH BUILT throughout.

They are good Hill Climbers, and being light in weight
there is seldom any trouble with the tyres.

10 h.p. Car. Price £270; with Governors £15 extra.

**The Motors are of the horizontal double cylinder type, and
being accurately balanced are very SILENT and FREE from
VIBRATION.**

Full particulars with Illustrations of 1903 Standard 6-h.p. and 10-h.p. Cars
on application to

THE "PICK" MOTOR Co., Ltd.,
STAMFORD.

We are Exhibiting at Crystal Palace.
Jan. 30 to Feb. 7, 1903. Stands 118-119.

Plate 17: Advertisement for the Pick Cars, from *The Car*, issue no. 37 (February 4, 1903)

That the Pick Motor Company was successful at this time, despite the underlying tension between Pick and the board, cannot be denied. Pick premises at 5 Blackfriars Street had been expanded into adjacent buildings during 1899 to provide for the growth in cycle manufacture, but now further expansion was needed. About two acres of land between Blackfriars Street and St Leonard's Street was acquired and a completely new factory was erected by John Woolston, a local builder, to plans by Stamford architect Joseph Ward. New plant and machinery was installed to produce as much as possible on the premises; chassis, bodies, engine and gearboxes, upholstery. Certain items would, of

Plate 18: Henry Tryon, Pick's test-driver, at the wheel of a 1903 10 h.p. car in the Blackfriar's Works yard. *Motoring Illustrated* (Saturday 27 June 1903), p. 118

course, have to be bought in, the carburettors, by Longuemare, and the electrical components for example. The *Stamford Mercury*'s reporter paid a visit to the works soon after completion in 1903 and wrote:

> Some fifty cars are at present in course of construction, varying from 4½ to 24 horse power. The increasing importance of the manufactory to a town like Stamford, and the extent of the work turned out, may be gauged from the fact that the number of men employed at the commencement had grown to upwards of 100, and overtime has been general from the start.[22]

The differences between Pick and the board came to a head during 1903. The last straw as far as Pick was concerned was the withdrawal of the company's two entrants in the Royal Automobile Club's 1000 Miles Reliability Trial. Pick was to have driven a four-seater, Henry Tryon, son of one of the directors, a two-seater. Pick was convinced of the possibility of doing well, and was conscious of the publicity value in taking part. In a fit of pique he borrowed the four-seater and took himself and three companions off to conduct his own reliability trial. The car behaved perfectly: as Pick said later 'the engine was never touched, not so much as a screw received attention'. On his return to the works he strongly expressed his opinion of the directors for withdrawing from the official trial and for his pains was suspended.[23]

In the meantime Henry Tryon took the 6 h.p. two-seater into third place in Class E at the Automobile Club speed trials in Southport. This was probably the first taste of racing success for the young man, who was shortly to leave Stamford and join Napiers as test driver. In 1907 he was a member of S. F. Edge's team when Edge broke the 24 hour distance record at Brooklands a few days before the official opening of the track. At the opening meeting Tryon won the Marcel Renault Memorial Plate for Napier. The following year he secured the 50 mile flying start record in the Napier before a burst tyre caused the car to leave the track and fly over the paddock road before embedding itself on the earth. Tryon survived to serve Napiers for fifty years followed by a further ten years as consultant. He died in 1965 aged 83.

What happened to the Pick Motor Company next is unclear. The firm exhibited as usual at the Crystal Palace Motor Show in February 1904 and in April was one of the forty three firms listed as having secured space for the following year's show to be held at Olympia. However, by the end of September advertisements were appearing in the local papers for 'Pick's Motor Works, St Martin's, Stamford'. Whether Pick resigned or was sacked is not recorded. He was now aged 37. With capital of just £285 and a £100 loan he started over again using his old title 'J. H. Pick and Co.' He found premises at 11 High Street, St Martin's, opposite the George Hotel, with a workshop at the rear where he installed secondhand machinery and a forge. With help from his brother Walter and several men who had followed him from Blackfriars Street he was back in business.[24]

Pick's old firm, now under the management of F. D. Tryon, changed its name to the Blackfriars' Motor and Engineering Works. Production of the Pick cars ceased and Tryon took on the agency for a curious American vehicle, the Orient Buckboard. Tryon's enterprise was short lived and by 1906 the firm had closed down.

What had gone wrong with Pick and Co.? It may be that the company was not as financially well founded from the beginning as it might have been and the expense incurred in building a totally new factory with all the plant and machinery were more than it could bear. However, if the reported growth in orders was correct, expansion was essential to cope with it. The disposal of the cycle manufactory in 1902 was an important loss but would have contributed only a small part of the total loss. Was there a lack of responsibility on the part of the directors who were accountable for the business side of the undertaking? Although the firm seems to have been successful, if judged by the numbers of cars being produced, one wonders if they were being produced profitably? There certainly seems to have been a lack of understanding of their works manager, whose engineering knowledge was the only saleable commodity they had. Did the friction between Pick and the board merely bring matters to a head, so that the end was inevitable from the outset? A sad state of affairs considering the remarks in the *Stamford Mercury* only a short time before.

24

The PICK cars.

For Particulars, apply
THE PICK MOTOR Co., Ltd. STAMFORD.

Double Cylinder 10 h.p. Tonneau Body Car.
PRICE £290 complete.

Sole Agents for London & District
FRANK F. WELLINGTON, Ltd.,
151 & 152, Wardour Street, LONDON, W.

Agents for Ireland
JOHN HUTTON, SONS & CO.,
115, Summer Hill, DUBLIN.

The PICK cars.

Double Cylinder 6 h.p. Voiturette.
PRICE £175 complete.
Awarded the bronze medal at the Southport Trials October 2 & 3, 1903.

Plate 19: advertisement for Pick Cars from J. E. C. Potter's *Stamford Almanack and Directory* for 1904, *Stamford Museum*

25

Plate 20: Superb 1903 photograph of the Pick Motor Company works in Gas Lane, Stamford, *Stamford Museum*

The factory was sold off and purchased by J. E. C. Potter and Son, a successful local commercial printing firm which still occupies it.

Charles Gray seems to have been Pick's only ally, for when he came to set up on his own account again it was Gray, his partner at the time of the founding of the Pick Motor Co., who loaned him £100 to help with the financing of his new business. It was also Gray and his son who had accompanied Pick on the unofficial 1,000 mile trial which brought about his leaving his old firm.[25]

After leaving Blackfriars Street, Pick was free once more to follow his own inclinations and was soon at work on a new chassis with a four cylinder vertical engine. It was not fully developed when he opened in St Martin's, so to tide things over for his men he took on any kind of repairs and light general engineering work he could get. He sold petrol, tyres and accessories in what had in effect become Stamford's first motor garage. He also found time to prepare an unsuccessful patent application for a cultivator. When the new chassis was completed in 1906, a smart modern two-seater body built by Hayes and Son of Stamford was mounted on it.

Plate 21: Another view of the 1903 Pick Motor Company Works in Gas Lane, Stamford. Stamford Museum

28

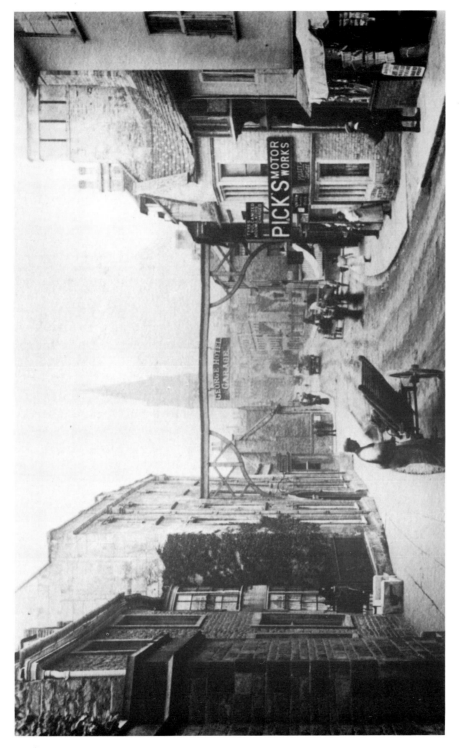

Plate 22: High Street, St Martin's, Stamford, *c*.1908, showing Pick's Motor Works at No. 11, conveniently opposite the George Hotel. *Stamford Museum*

29

Plate 23: Charles Gray when mayor of Stamford in 1901: Pick's only supporter on the Pick Motor Company board, *Phillips Collection, Stamford Town Hall*

In July 1907 *The Autocar* reviewed the car, first commenting that the low price gave the 'impression of the impossibility to produce a satisfactory car for the money. However, on looking over the chassis, we found that, although rough in places, there was no scamping of the important working parts.' The engine was rated at 12-14 h.p. with a bore and stroke of 86 mm. with four separately cast cylinders and opposed valves, that is with the inlet valves on one side and the exhaust valves on the other. 'The engine', said *The Autocar*, 'runs without vibration. The steering was very easy and is of new design.' Transmission was through a fibre faced cone clutch and two speed gearbox with propeller shaft drive to a live axle. Braking was by a pedal operated transmission brake on the propeller shaft and a hand brake to two rear wheel brake drums. *The Automotor Journal* described the rack and pinion steering gear, which operated through a universal jointed steering shaft, as 'unusual and peculiar' in being situated in front of the axle. The report concluded that 'in this vehicle, the company have the nucleus of a good little car, and with the addition of a third speed it should prove an excellent little vehicle for town and touring work'.[26]

Just before the launch of the new car the firm was given the name 'New Pick Motor Company'. To provide production space Pick took over the coachbuilder's workshops recently vacated by Hayes and Son on the corner of Barnack Road and High Street, St Martin's. Hayes and Son continued to supply Pick with bodies from their Scotgate works until the First World War ended production. A range of models with differing body styles and engine sizes was offered and with improved sales: in 1908 *fifty* cars were ordered by the Earl's Court Motor Company. The new company was established as a flourishing concern.

Plate 24: Pick's Motor Works, 11, High Street, St Martin's, Stamford, *c.*1908, across from the George Hotel. *Stamford Museum*

Pick's first exhibition with his new cars was at the Agricultural Halls Show in March 1908. Two cars were on display, a two seater and a four seater. He seems to have heeded *The Autocar* review of the previous year. The engines were now developing 14-16 h.p. with a bore and stroke of 90 mm. x 100 mm. and were equipped with three speed gear boxes.[27] Two years later, in 1910, Pick published his first illustrated catalogue, complete with prices: the two seater 170 guineas, the four seater 190 guineas, both finished in 'Napier Green, suitably lined and trimmed'. The catalogue also shows two versions of the racy looking New Pick Semi-Racer, two seater sports 'well capable of 50 miles per hour'. A rolling chassis with a nine feet wheel base, presumably suitable for all variations, cost 144 guineas. Priced parts lists were also included.[28] In 1911 the original engine with four separately cast cylinders was replaced with a monobloc engine with the same bore of 90 mm., but Pick had increased the stroke to 127mm. and the engine was now developing 16-18 h.p. All the valves were on one side operated by a single camshaft.

A new and ambitious range of vehicles was announced in 1912. There were two types, each based on a single chassis layout with the new 16-18 h.p. monobloc engine. The 'Standard' two and four seater models remained much as they had in the previous catalogue, but Pick now introduced the sporty 'Torpedo' models. Also to be had in two or four seater models, they had a round radiator which gave them a barrel shaped bonnet. With the front wings rounded like the bonnet and with a spare Stepney wheel and tyre fitted alongside the driver, they had quite a dashing appearance. In addition a Landaulette or Taxi and a Delivery van were offered on a more robust chassis. Pick confidently claimed that his cars were 'the acme of simplicity, quietness of running, and ease of control' and modestly asserted that 'there is no other Car on the market to compare with it in price and reliability'. There may have been some truth in that because several cars of this period still survive.[29]

Car production did not cease immediately at the outbreak of the First World War in 1914 but appears to have continued until the middle of 1915. Pick was certainly advertising his 20 h.p. models in the *Stamford Mercury* until the 25th June that year. A motoring writer from *The Autocar* came to Stamford

> in frightful weather to inspect the entrails of the new 20 h.p. Pick... The workmanship is good in the parts that matter, though the engine is not polished up to dazzle you if you incautiously open the bonnet. The parts that are made in Stamford are well made of good stuff, and the bought details come from good firms – the springs from Woodhead's, the worm from Wrigley's, and so on, while it has an English lighting dynamo and a speedometer, the latter let in flush with dash . . . The big Pick has an engine measuring 95 mm. x 127 mm. and its top gear is 3 to 1. When it is travelling at 50 m.p.h., its engine is barely exceeding 1750 r.p.m., and there is no pother under the bonnet; it suggests neither vibration or noise, and it is really well sprung.

He concluded that it was 'extraordinarily good value'. The purpose of the author's visit was to compare the five seater selling for £250 with an equivalent light car carrying four and priced at £200. 'A light car', he wrote, 'with a load of four persons has to be very low geared, and it cannot hope to approach 50 m.p.h. under any circumstances; at its maximum of, say, 30-40 m.p.h. it is nearing 3,000 r.p.m., is making a great flurry and noise, and is in a state of violent vibration. Per contra, the big Pick weighs about a ton and probably averages no more than twenty miles to the gallon.' He therefore concluded that 'the big car is easily the more attractive proposition of the two'. However, he warned that the upkeep would be 'considerably higher' and that the price difference 'of only £50 is no index to the divergence in respective upkeeps'. In other words, the bigger the car the higher the upkeep. How true![30]

At the end of the war Pick found himself in a difficult situation. Although his works had been turned over to war work, they were not taken under Government control as a controlled establishment . He was therefore not eligible

Plate 25: New Pick two seater of 1911 in New Zealand, photographed when it was owned and restored by L. Briggs. *Clem MacLachan*

Plate 26: The same car, as now owned by Mrs. W. Bryson in New Zealand. *Clem MacLachan*

Plates 27 and 28: two photographs of one of the two Pick cars imported by Mr Mulligan of Maronan, New Zealand. This 1910-11 two seater is similar to the Briggs' car (plate 25). See the account of 'Survivors' on pages 48-50.

Plate 29: A 1913 photograph of the late George Knight of Great Casterton at the wheel of his 1910-11 New pick 'Racer'. *Stamford Museum, original loaned by R. Knight*

Plate 30: Frederick Wilson, Pick's test driver, on an outing to Wakerley Woods with his wife, Annie, and her family in a 1914 Special four seater Touring Car. Sitting on Annie's lap is daughter Millicent who generously gave the photograph.

Plate 31: The New Pick Torpedo Four Seater of about 1912, fitted with Stepney Wheel.
Stamford Museum, original loaned by T. Harding

for either subsidies or post war assistance to replace machinery worn out on munitions production. This may have been a major consideration in his decision not to return to car production for the time being. It did mean, though, that Pick missed out on the brief post-war demand for motor cars, which created a period of intense competition between makers. Greatly increased production and large price reductions (Morris cut his by a fifth) forced many small manufacturers to amalgamate or to close down so that by the early nineteen twenties the industry was dominated by Morris and Austin. After the war Morris was looking for an engine and gearbox supplier for his new models and negotiated with several manufacturers. In an attempt to revive his moribund business Pick said he approached him with an offer to produce the engines. Morris turned him down on the quite reasonable grounds of insufficient capacity. In the event Morris used an American designed engine built by the Hotchkiss company of Coventry.

However, Jack Pick was not a man to stand idle. While his factory was busy with the war effort he still found time to plan for peace time and turned to the needs of agriculture. A patent application for a 'motor for tilling' was published in August 1918 and the prototype vehicle was entered for the 1919 tractor trials organised by the Society of Motor Manufacturers and Traders.[31] The event was held over four days in September at South Carlton, near Lincoln, on an area of land which gave a good variation of soil types and conditions. Among the major makers taking part were F.I.A.T., International and Fordson. The Pick was accompanied by entrants from two other Stamford engineering firms; Blackstone and Co. Ltd with two tractors, one wheeled and one tracked, and the Martin's Cultivator Company with a wheeled tractor and a self-propelled plough.

36

Plate 32: The Pick Motor Company's entrant for the tractor trials held at South Carlton, near Lincoln, in 1919. The unconventional (even by contemporary standards) layout of the controls can be clearly seen. The driver is Bob Sissons.
Stamford Museum, original loaned by C. Davis

Plate 33: The length of the Pick 1919 tractor trials entry is accentuated, in this view from the radiator side, by the plough attached to the rear
Museum of English Rural Life

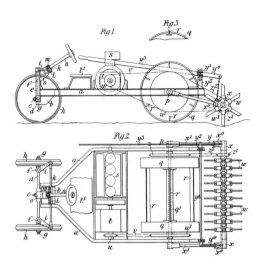

Plate 34: Original patent for Pick's 'Improvements in or connected with Motor Tractors for Tilling and other purposes' (no. 117,699, 1918, from the published patent)

The Pick tractor is the most distinctive in appearance of all the competing machines. It is one of the three-wheeled variety, built very low, and is fitted with a four cylinder engine driving, through a cone clutch, a transmission gear which is inclined to give nine changes of speed in either forward or reverse directions, the ratios varying 18.75 to 1 to 41.5 to 1. The final drive is by roller chain and spur wheels to a back axle on which are mounted a pair of wheels 30ins. in diameter by 6ins. wide. When ploughing, these two wheels are connected by cross bars which convert the two wheels into one open roller, or cage. While it has excellent adhesion properties it was noted that they had a tendency to choke up, particularly when working on heavy clay land, or even moist loam. The machine is not spring mounted, and only one brake is provided. The general design of the machine, with its radiators disposed along the side, is such that access to the working parts is rather difficult. Intending purchasers should enquire as to the availability of spare parts for this tractor.[32]

The machine did indeed have a distinctive appearance. It stood only about four feet high and was approximately eleven feet long. The driver sat amidships in front of the 30 h.p. petrol engine which was fully enclosed, in what looked like an oil drum, with the fuel tank set behind above the rear wheels. Alongside the driver were the two cooling radiators. The single enclosed front wheel was housed inside a turntable steerable through a gearbox at the bottom of the steeply raked steering column. A gear change lever, looking as though it had come from a railway signal box, was on the driver's right, a second lever, for raising and lowering the plough on this strange machine, stood behind on the left. It must have taken some agility on the part of the operator to slide the cross bars between the rear wheels to convert them into an open roller.

38

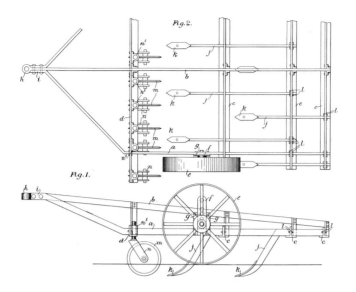

Plate 35: Original patent for Pick's 'Improvements in Cultivators, Harrows and like Land-Tilling Implements' (patent 186,128, 1922, from the published patent)

It cannot be said that the trials were a great success for Pick. On the first day of ploughing the tractor suffered a broken gear and was out of action for most of the day. Next day the Pick's ploughing test was delayed when overheating set fire to woodwork, possibly the floor. The trials judges were not impressed.

> In general construction most of the machines are perfectly sound, but it should be noted that in some cases access to parts requiring attention for adjustments, etc, has not always been kept in view by the designer. This is particularly true of the Pick. The tendency for the Pick to take fire in the event of serious and accidental overheating can easily be overcome by eliminating all woodwork. This tractor is obviously in an experimental stage. Owing to the breaking of a gearwheel it did practically no work on the heavy land. On the light land it did some fairly good work, but as a result of rain the driving drum became clogged and the machine stopped. [33]

Pick had been no more successful in solving the problem of clogging on wet land than he had been twenty five years earlier. One wonders what possessed him to design, let alone build, such a contraption. He could not have been unaware of previous work on this type of machine. He must have known of, and probably had seen, the demonstration given by Don Albone of his highly successful three-wheeled Ivel Agricultural Tractor at Priory Farm, Uffington Road, Stamford, in August 1902.[34] This was the machine which may be said to have set the standard for the modern tractor, light, manoeuvrable and above all simple to operate. Nor can Pick have been unaware of current thinking in tractor design when most British makers followed generally accepted automotive practices.

39

Plate 36: Illustration of the Pick Farm Tractor of 1920
from the company's catalogue, *Stamford Museum*

At £550 the Pick was not the most expensive tractor taking part but when tested against a dynamometer, as all the entrants were, it was one of the least efficient. The Alldays (at £630), with its 30 h.p. engine, showed a drawbar horse power of 15 with a capital cost of £19 per 100*lb.* of drawbar pull. By comparison the Pick produced only 8 drawbar horse power at a capital cost of £30 per 100*lb.* of drawbar pull. However, the Alldays' weight of three tons made it more suitable for road haulage rather than use as an agricultural tractor. Even so, at two and a quarter tons the Pick was a real heavy-weight alongside the Fordson. The latter was a more efficient machine altogether. It tipped the scales at a little over one and a quarter tons and although it only produced 6¼ h.p. on the drawbar the equivalent capital cost was £18 15*s.* per 100*lb.* and the price was a mere £280. It had its drawbacks, of course:

> The Fordson's inclination to rear is a decided disadvantage and might be serious on some kinds of land, particularly stony ground, whilst the absence of brakes makes it a most unsuitable machine for use on the road or sloping land with any wheeled vehicle or implement behind it.[35]

Despite these dangerous attributes the Fordson was to become the most popular tractor on British farms. Indeed, more than 7,000 were already in use and its general layout was followed by most other manufacturers.

Another tractor trial was organised the following year, 1920, by the Society of Motor Manufacturers and Traders in co-operation with the Royal Agricultural Society of England. The venue was on some 600 acres of varied ground at Aisthorpe and adjoining Scampton aerodrome near Lincoln and took place over ten days at the end of September. Among the 40 or so manufacturers entered were once more vehicles from Pick, Blackstone and Co., Ltd and Martin's Cultivator Company.

Pick's entry was a more conventional vehicle than the previous year's. Conventional in the sense that it had four wheels, one at each corner in the Fordson tradition, with the driver sitting behind the engine above the rear wheels. It had a 20 h.p. four cylinder paraffin engine running at 800 r.p.m., three forward gears and reverse with a cone clutch. Complete and in running order it weighed two tons. The front wheels were three feet diameter, the rear wheels four feet diameter by twelve inches wide. As the trials report states:

> ...the chief feature of this tractor is the driving wheel. It is built on lines which make it impossible to clog, and grips the land without spikes and strakes. Also it is built to meet road regulations for hauling. The patentee claims that the machines can go straight off the road on to the land and, without adjustments, commence ploughing. The market price of the 'Pick' is £450, and threshing pulley is provided.[36]

As in the previous trial misfortune struck. The Pick, which had performed 'very creditably', suffered an accident while off the trials field and was unable to complete the contest; consequently no performance details were published.

Despite the failure of his tractors at the two trials, Pick issued a leaflet detailing and extolling the advantages of his tractors, but whether he sold any is doubtful. In 1923 he entered into partnership with Charles Miles, a local timber merchant, to re-finance the company. With a nominal capital of £8,000 in £1 shares the firm was registered as the Pick Motor Company Limited. The directors were J. H. Pick, Charles Miles snr., the chairman, and Charles Miles jnr.

A glossy catalogue illustrated with artist's impressions of the firm's new model cars superimposed on photographs of nearby Burghley Park was prepared. Four models were advertised; an open two seater priced at £365, an open four seater at £385, a coupé at £410, and the two-door saloon, £450. The body panels on all models were of heavy gauge aluminium, 'which ensures no rusting to raise the paint', on an ash frame. Both the coupé and the saloon were 'designed with a V front for less wind resistance, and a V back to avoid suction'. Another feature the company impressed on the prospective purchaser that should not be overlooked were the 'Pick Patent Perfect Seats' [which] 'are fitted to these bodies, these being moveable, and can be taken out in five minutes for sleeping accommodation or carrying luggage'. A precursor of the camper van perhaps.[37]

They were large cars (the saloon was nearly eleven feet long overall) with slow revving engines based on the old 1914 power unit and uprated to 22 b.h.p. at 800 r.p.m. *The Autocar* road tested one of the sports models and declared that those who have a preference for the large engine over the small high speed engine have in the Pick an 'opportunity to gratify their wishes at a very reasonable outlay'. It is, they said, 'the equivalent of seven league boots, and covers the ground at a fine pace with the engine ticking quietly round'; at 40 m.p.h. the engine revolutions were a mere 1,000 per minute. The three speed gear box was of heavy construction, the gears being big and large toothed with very high ratios – 2 to 1, 4½ to 1, 8½ to 1. 'Undoubtedly the highest geared

Plate 37: Huskinson and Fane, Invicta agents, purchased St Martin's Garage from
Charles Miles in 1929. They sold out to A. T. Cross in 1932
Stamford Museum, original loaned by P. Cross

modern touring automobile produced today. It recalls the days of the old type
Continental chain-driven productions, not in performance but in gearing. At
10-12 m.p.h. on top gear – one can count the beats of the engine, so slow does it
turn over at this speed, and herein lies a marked feature of its fascination'.[38] The
high gearing which enabled the car to cruise so smoothly and effortlessly was
really its undoing, as the acceleration must have been tediously sluggish.

This type of car was no longer fashionable, and the Pick was decidedly old
fashioned, in looks and performance. Competition was coming from smaller,
lighter cars with lower capacity higher revving engines which made 'a great flurry
and noise' and were encouraged by the introduction of '£1 per horse power tax'.
In 1922 Herbert Austin had introduced his famous Austin Seven, which was
quickly followed by the Morris Minor and the Ford Eight. As the post war boom
came to an end and depression set in, demand for high horse-power cars faded
and only the larger and securely established makers who were producing a range
of models were able to survive. Even Austin found it hard. Those manufacturers
who did attempt to market new large engined cars, such as Vauxhall with their
25/70, model got into difficulties. This was the climate into which Pick launched
his new models. No sales figures survive, and Pick gave no clues, but it is
doubtful if any cars were sold.

Plate 38: St Martin's Garage soon after it had been purchased by Charles Miles. Standing outside from left to right are: A. T. Cross, who acquired the concern in 1932 and was the father of Peter, who loaned this and other photographs to Stamford Museum; Charles Walpole; Fred Clough, coach painter; and Charlie Williams

In January 1925 the Pick Motor Co. Ltd went into voluntary liquidation and on the 21st a sale of all stock and machinery took place in the St Martin's works. The record of prices reached is incomplete but what has survived makes interesting reading. Among the more than 800 lots were three 22.5 h.p. cars: a yellow and black coupé complete with electric lighting and starter reached £180, a two-seater sports without lighting or starter went for £50, and a second coupé, unpainted and untrimmed, was knocked down for £60. Apart from these, a Pratt's petrol pump with a 500 gallon tank containing an estimated 175 gallons of petrol sold for £80 and the workshop machinery fetched under £500; bidding seems to have been less than enthusiastic. Three chassis went for ten shillings each, a 1909 Pick chassis 'in running order' was sold for £3. Another chassis complete with 22.5 h.p. engine, gearbox and both axles, a separate engine and gear box and a 35 h.p. tractor were also included. One wonders where it all went.[39]

The principal purchaser was the chairman of the Pick Motor Company, Charles Miles. He took over the premises at 23 St Martin's and by 4 February was advertising as Miles and Co., Automobile Engineers. Later the same year the name of the premises became St Martin's Garage, a title it retained until the late 1980s. By 1929 the garage was operated by Messrs Huskinson and Fane but by 1933 Archibald Cross was the proprietor.

Plate 39: Among this collection of cars inside St Martin's Garage are an Austin Seven, Morgan, Standard, Morris, Vauxhall and perhaps an Invicta
Stamford Museum, original loaned by P. Cross

What of John Henry Pick? He retained 11 St Martin's, where twenty one years earlier he had begun his second motor car works, and at the front he opened a greengrocer's shop. He was now fifty eight years old. At the rear he maintained a small workshop in which he kept his hand in with small engineering jobs. In 1933 the *Stamford and Rutland News* reported that Ransomes, Sims and Jefferies Ltd., of Ipswich, were to carry out a field trial of a new type potato digger designed by Pick but nothing seems to have come of it He returned to the obscurity from which he rose, making a small but steady living until he died on 4th January 1954 aged 87.

Local tradition compares 'Jack' Pick favourably with William Morris and holds that Pick could have been another Lord Nuffield. Indeed, there are some similarities. Morris too set up as a cycle repairer, in Oxford in 1893, and turned to making bicycles and later motor cycles. He then became a motor car agent

Plate 40: Pick's workforce in about 1915, *Stamford Museum, original loaned by C. Davis*

and repairer. In 1910 he made his own light car. Here the similarities end. Morris, unlike Pick, favoured buying in engines, gearboxes, axles, wheels, and even bodies, it being cheaper and more reliable than producing his own. Morris, unlike Pick, was an entrepreneur with the ability to raise the large sums of money required to finance his enterprises. Pick on the other hand was a hands on engineer who, apart from Charles Gray, who seems to have been his firmest supporter but was no marketing man, found himself under the control of others who held the purse strings.

So could Stamford have become another Cowley? Pick certainly had the financial backing that was required to set up a volume production factory employing around a hundred men in 1903. It was certainly feasible geographically speaking: Blackstone and Co., one of the country's leading diesel engine builders, had been in the town since 1837. It must be said, however, that Pick was not one of the easiest men to work with. He stood for and was elected to the Borough Council but it was a short lived career. The outspoken manner and earthy language cannot have endeared him to those who tried to maintain the niceties of either the boardroom or the council chamber. He campaigned for the town to have a proper swimming pool, to end the dangers of bathing in the river Welland, but fell out with his fellow councillors over the siting of it. His love of sport, which got him into trouble as a young man in Clipsham, was put to practical use when he opened his St Martin's works. He recruited into his workforce several young footballers, especially from among the unemployed of Northampton, who were given time off to play for the Stamford Town football club, 'The Daniels'. He was particularly proud when 'his' team won the 1st Division of the Northamptonshire Football League in the 1911/12 season. And it was Jack Pick who was instrumental in raising the money to pay for the materials used to build the grandstand at the Daniels' ground.

He was a stubborn man with a determination to have things his way and is alleged to have punningly described himself as 'pickheaded'; and perhaps that is the clue to his lack of success. Not that he was a failure, far from it. Any man with only an elementary education who can raise himself from the ranks of the ordinary working man to become a successful creative engineer and motor manufacturer in his own right cannot be considered a failure.

Plate 41, above: The Pick radiator badge, *Stamford Museum*
Plate 42, opposite: Part of Pick's workshop equipment was still in use when this photograph was taken in St Martin's Garage in the late nineteen thirties
Stamford Museum, original loaned by P. Cross
Plate 43, opposite: Pick Voiturette, CT 174, during the 1961 Veteran Car Rally, which was part of Stamford's Quincentenary celebrations. Seated on the car in Broad Street is the then owner Ted Steeper. Standing each side are Walter Pick and his daughter Mrs Dodman, *Stamford Museum*

SURVIVORS

There is, as far as the author knows, no record of the number of vehicles produced by the Pick Motor Company in either of its two forms. Only two complete cars survive in Great Britain and four in New Zealand. Quite a creditable number considering the relatively short history of the firm.

The earliest of the surviving cars is CT 174, a Voiturette which has been dated by the Veteran Car Club to 1901. The late Percy Cox made some notes on this car after seeing a photograph of it in a local newspaper in 1965. As a child Mr Cox lived in Grove Cottage, Wothorpe Road, Stamford.

> When my sister and I were small we rode in the corner seats at the small back door in the centre back panel. When we outgrew those seats they were removed and replaced by a flat panel. Hand brake applied to the rear wheel treads, extra passenger weight and bouncy roads caused variable braking. I drove this car when I was about 13 (1912-13) with no more tuition than just watching as a passenger. Flat belt drive to a counter shaft, chain to rear axle, two forward gears, no reverse. Starting handle had to be threaded between the front wheel spokes. Engine lubrication was by a hand pump on dash board. No instruments. If you tried to change gear without using the clutch, the belt either broke or came off. The owner then said, 'right that's enough.'

During a conversation with the author, octogenarian David 'Harry' Islip, who knew Mr Cox and his family, added

> The owner at this time [1912-13] was Charlie Porter, a crank inspector at Blackstones, who courted his wife in the car. He garaged it in a shed at the rear of Grove Cottage in Wothorpe Road. When it came to the end of its road he used it to drive a lathe. When Charlie died, just after the Second World War, his widow let a chap called Tommy Gilbert restore the car to some use and then it was sold.

A report in the *Barnsley Chronicle* of 20th January 1984 describes how Alan Booth stumbled across the car in a scrap yard between Wakefield and Leeds in 1947 and bought it for £25.

> I thought what a splendid idea it would be to restore it. I opened the bonnet and found things pretty rough underneath. But I put some petrol in and a battery and it started almost straight away so I was able to drive it home to Cundy Cross. It was in pretty rough shape generally and needed a lot of work to clean it up. The carburettor and petrol tank were all of brass and the mudguards were wood. I sent it to a coach painter in Sheffield for the body work doing and, in fact, they didn't charge me anything because they were so pleased to restore such a car.

It took part in the Brighton Run and made a trip to Paris in 1950. Mr Booth sold the car for £250 in 1954. The subsequent owners were: A. E. 'Ted' Steeper (1954-64, during this period the car took part in the Stamford Quincentenary

Rally in 1961. Ted Steeper was photographed with Walter Pick, the builder's brother.); Michael G. Jackson (1964-65); Jim Parrish (1965-67); Mr and Mrs J. Garrett (1967-1984. In 1973 the car was a participant in the Fanfare for Europe Motor Rally from London to Brussels); Mr and Mrs N. Lord (1984 to the present). The car has been a regular entrant in the Brighton Run since it was extensively restored by the present owners. Whether this is the same car that the youthful Percy Cox drove in 1912 and that Charlie Porter did his courting in cannot be conclusively proven, but need it be? Let's keep the romance alive!

Plate 44: The 1912 Doctor's Coupé owned by R. H. S. Long, *Stamford Museum*

The second Pick survivor is AF 174, a Doctor's Coupé of 1912. This car does not have the romantic background of CT 174. Discovered in pieces in a loft near Bradford it was purchased by R. H. S. Long in 1962 after it had been rebuilt and restored. In 1963 the car was driven from Scunthorpe to Bognor Regis to take part in a F.I.V.A. event, a round trip of approximately five hundred miles. It subsequently took part in several Hull–Scarborough Runs but, apart from an appearance in a TV play in 1969, the car has been little used and is displayed at the owner's garage near Scunthorpe.

The Pick Motor Co. exported to a number of countries in the British Empire but in only two have any shown up. In Australia John Jewel has the remains of a *c*.1905 chain driven Pick. One wonders if others may be languishing in any of the scrap yards which have already yielded up many interesting transport relics.

New Zealand is surprisingly rich in Pick survivors. Clem MacLachan of Ashburton has provided information on six cars. The numbers quoted appear on the respective flywheels. All the cars date from the 1912-14 period. No. 677 is owned by J. Simpson but is dismantled. No. 687 is owned by A. B. Thomas, also dismantled. The radiator from this car is in the Museum of Transport and Technology, Western Springs. No. 690 is owned by C. R. Maclachan and has been restored using the engine from no. 677 and the gearbox from no. 687. No. 693 is owned by W. R. Bryson and has been restored but is needing an engine and gearbox rebuild. No. 695 is owned by L. Everett and has been restored.

Clem MacLachan reports that the late father of Felix Mulligan of Maronan owned two Picks. One, purchased in 1912, the second in about 1920. This was a 1914 model which was apparently due to be shipped from London when war broke out. It stayed in a warehouse at the docks until the war ended and it could be sent to New Zealand. Although somewhat out of date it still cost Mr Mulligan £300. One of these cars was dismantled and may be one of the cars described above, the other is now owned by N. F. Clarke. The Maclachan and Everett cars are both regularly rallied.

Plate 45: John Henry Pick in later life.
Stamford Museum, original loaned by John Henry's grandson P. Brandreth.

NOTES

[1] In the Autumn of 1946 the *Lincolnshire, Rutland and Stamford Mercury* (hereafter 'LRSM') published a series of good anecdotal articles by John Sindall based on interviews with Jack Pick. They formed a starting point for the research for this book and provided much of the background to the Pick story.

[2] Patent No. 8044. 1894.

[3] Patent No. 19,736. 1894.

[4] Sindall.

[5] Copy of this agreement found in the Stamford office of McArthur Group Ltd., formerly Charles Gray Ltd. The original in the possession of Mr Peter Pledger.

[6] LRSM (13 August 1897).

[7] LRSM (28 January 1898).

[8] *Stamford and Rutland News* (hereafter SRN) (17 March 1899).

[9] LRSM (31 March 1899); Sindall.

[10] SRN (28 June 1900); LRSM (31 August 1900); Sindall.

[11] *The Antique Automobile*, St John C. Nixon (London, 1956).

[12] LRSM (23 November 1900); *Motor Car Journal* (24 November 1900); *Autocar* (1 December 1900).

[13] *Stamford Post* (5 April 1901).

[14] Sindall.

[15] *Autocar* (11 May 1901); *Motor Car Journal* (25 May 1901).

[16] *Carriage Builder's Journal* (March 1901).

[17] *Automotor Journal* (March 1902).

[18] SRN (20 February 1902).

[19] *Autocar* (18 October, 1 November, 8 November 1902).

[20] Reminiscences of W. H. Edinborough. LRSM (3 February 1939).

[21] *The Motor* (11 February 1903).

[22] LRSM (1 May 1903).

[23] Sindall.

[24] Sindall.

[25] Sindall.

[26] *Autocar* (13 July 1907); *Automotor Journal* (28 March 1908).

[27] *The Car Illustrated* (25 March 1908); *Automotor Journal* (28 March 1908).

[28] New Pick Motor Company catalogue 1910.

[29] Pick Motor Company catalogue 1912.

[30] *Autocar* (2 January 1915).

[31] Patent No.

[32] Trials Judges' report.

[33] Trials Judges' report.

[34] Trials Judges' report.

[35] Trials Judges' report.

[36] Trials Judges' report.

[37] Pick Motor Company catalogue 1924.

[38] *Autocar* (30 March 1923); *The Motor* (24 July 1923).

[39] Annotated Sale catalogue in Stamford Museum collection.

THE SPORTS PICK ON THE ROAD
Extract from *The Motor* (July 24, 1923), 1061-62

The name of Pick takes one back to the old days of belt drive, when this make was of the single lunger type and it seems hardly possible that the present model can be the product of the same designer. Yet this is the case, and, what is more, certain features are even as unconventional as the old belt-drive car would be in this era.

Rated at 22.5 h.p., the new sporting model Pick is a return to the types that had big capacity, low-speed power units, and even at 40 m.p.h. the revs. are only approximately 1,000 per minute. From this it will be gathered that even for the present-day super-efficient type of motorcar the gearing is abnormally high – two and one eighth to one on top, four and a quarter to one on second, eight and a half to one on bottom and ten to 1 on reverse! It is undoubtedly the highest-geared modern touring automobile produced today. Such, however, is the courage of the designer's convictions in his product, and we were indeed very sceptical on taking over the car for a run of 100 miles.

The four-cylinder, three-bearing monobloc engine is of the side valve type, with a bore of 95 mm and a stroke of 127 mm, 3,601 c.c., and is, to all outward appearances, conventional in every way, and so it is internally. A novel yet simple method of lubrication is, however, employed; an archimedean screw, operated from the camshaft, conveying the oil from the sump, after which it flows via channels to the main bearings and to the troughs. The right hand operated gearbox is a massive and separate unit, while the drive thereto from the engine is through a fibre-faced cone clutch, a few drops of oil on which successfully cures any tendency to fierceness. Drive and torque strains are taken by a triangulated member, and the open propeller shaft which conveys the power to the substantial overhead worm-driven differential axle has a Hardy flexible fabric universal joint at each end.

The suspension fore and aft is effected by means of semi-elliptic springs, and the brakes operate on the transmission and road wheels respectively.

To one accustomed to handling the conventionally geared car, the Pick indeed comes as a novel and fascinating experience. It recalls the days of the old type Continental chain-driven productions, not in performance but in gearing. At 10-12 m.p.h. on top gear is scarcely an exaggeration to say that one can count the beats of the engine, so slow does it turn over at this speed, and herein lies a marked feature of its fascination. At 30-40 m.p.h. it simply floats along, and, despite the fact that a straight-through exhaust was fitted, it is wonderfully quiet at this pace. Decelerating from the speed mentioned, the car still continues to float, and only a glance at the speedometer acquaints one with the fact that, with the foot off the accelerator, it is registering the limit laid down by law; but there it is, and it almost wants experiencing to believe it. Taking into consideration the gearing, the Pick has quite good acceleration, and 60 m.p.h. can very quickly be attained. Even then the engine does not rev. at more than 1,600 per minute.

The question, however, that we can hear being asked is, "Will it climb?" It apparently seems equal to all ordinary gradients on its 4 1/4 to one second gear, for anything up to 40 m.p.h. is possible. Whether it will negotiate hills in the nature of a 1 in 5 gradient with ease is a point we were unable to prove, as our route did not lay over country of this nature. Gradients like Fitzjohn's Avenue and White Hill, on the main

Henley-Maidenhead road, were taken at a very fast pace on second, and when in full swing any ordinary rise could be taken in its stride on top.

The suspension on the particular car we tried was open to some criticism on moderately rough roads, and there is no doubt that the addition of shock absorbers, which are contemplated as standard equipment, will very greatly improve the road-holding qualities and all-round comfort.

The brakes are progressive and smooth in action, although the larger drums now being fitted will even add to their efficiency. The hand-brake operation is of the push-on type.

Taking into consideration the size of the engine it is economical on petrol and oil, the fuel consumed working out at over 20 m.p.g.

In appearance the aluminium body is imposing, the 10-ft. wheelbase and the high running boards contributing to this end. The driving position is comfortable, the large, thin-rimmed steering wheel being so raked as not to require any stretching of the arms. The spare wheel is carried flush against the "cut-off" tail, and in the boot, which is capable of holding a considerable quantity of luggage, is a dickey seat.

The price of the two-seater is £342, and the four-seater sells at £362. The manufacturers are the Pick Motor Co., of Stamford, and the sole agents for London and the Home Counties are the Bryanston Garage, 45, Crawford, Place, London W.1.

Plate 46: The same car photographed on Stamford Meadows, *Stamford Museum.*

GUARANTEE.

~~~~~~

ON delivery to us, carriage paid, within Twelve Months from purchase, of any defective part, we guarantee to supply a duplicate of such part free, provided the defect is one of workmanship or of material, and is not caused by rough usage or neglect.

THE 'PICK' MOTOR CO.,
STAMFORD, LINCS.,
(ENGLAND).

Hints as to the Treatment

of the "Pick" Car. . . .

IF your Motor goes jerky, and does not pull up to power:—

SEE that your Sparking Plugs are clean and that all are firing.

SEE that you have plenty of lubrication.

SEE that the make and brake in Magneto are not sticking.

SEE that the Compression is good.

WHEN you let the Clutch in, and it does not take up smoothly, Oil it, or it might seize.

Misfiring. etc.

The signs of this are :—

Irregular pulling of the Car, or a noticeable loss of power and speed.

To remedy this :—

1.—Sparking Plugs should be examined, and kept dry and clean.

2.—Cable connections from Magneto to Plugs should be kept apart, to avoid a short circuit.

3.—Make and Brake on Magneto should be examined (especially after the Car has been standing a few days, more so in damp weather), to see that they do not stick.

4.—To make sure that all the Cylinders are firing, the Compression Taps should be opened (one at a time) when Engine is running. The explosion will then be noticeable, if the above items (Nos. 1, 2, and 3) are correct.

5.—Care should be taken to replace the Cables on their proper Terminals.

The Terminals on Magneto are marked 1, 2, 3, 4. The correct firing order of the Cylinders is 1, 2, 4, 3.

Switch.

It is advisable to notice that when the Engine is running, Switch should be on the off, and vice versa.

3

Should any of the above occur, it is advisable to put about three-quarters of a pint of Lubricating Oil direct into the Crank Chamber; this is done by removing the Plug provided for that purpose in the Crank Chamber.

Oil should run fairly freely through the Sight Feed Lubricator, and if it does not, the following should be examined:—

1.—The Exhaust Pressure Pipe, to see that it is clear; this should, in any case, be taken off and cleaned out occasionally.

2.—The Needle of the Sight Feed Lubricator may also get stopped: this can be removed by taking off the top of the Lubricator.

Cardan Shaft Joints and Bolts and Square Coupling.

These should be kept well greased, and during the first few weeks a little Oil should be applied to same about every 100 miles, and after a little wear it is occasionally advisable to tighten them. Invariably the want of lubrication will cause a squeak here, which can be heard distinctly when the Car is running.

Back Axle.

The Lubricant required for this should be slightly thinner than that used for the Gear-box, and could be obtained by mixing the Vasoleum Grease with good Lubricating Oil (two parts of Grease to one part of Oil), and the Back Axle Case kept almost full. The lid of the Axle Case should be removed for examination, and the Case filled up, if necessary, every 400 to 500 miles.

Carburettor.

Should an insufficient supply of Petrol be noticed, that is, if the Carburettor will not flood, the supply pipe should be examined, to see that it is clear and clean.

To make sure that the Petrol is getting into the Float Chamber of Carburettor, remove conical Cap on the top of the Filter, and see that the Float Valve is clear.

Should it be necessary to remove the Needle Valve, care should be taken in replacing it. The correct position, after screwing right up, will be arrived at by unscrewing 1½ turns.

N.B.—The Fan Belt should be kept tight.

Magneto Lubrication.

Two or three drops of Lubricating Oil, in holes provided for same, every 300 to 400 miles.

Lubrication.

Great care should be taken to see that this is well looked after, especially for the first 1,000 miles. The Engine should be kept slightly smoking at the exhaust pipe for this distance, and even after, it should be allowed to smoke occasionally, to ensure full power from Engine.

Results of Insufficient Lubrication.

1.—Failing power in Engine.

2.—Overheating of water.

3.—Occasional difficulty in starting Engine when hot.

4.—Loss of Compression, through Pistons being dry.

5.—Irregular running of the Engine.

Adjustment of Back Brakes.

These should be adjusted to pull on equally on both sides by screwing the joints up on the Connecting Rods.

Adjustment of Foot Brake.

This is done at the Connecting Rod (between the Brake Pedal and the Brake Arm), by loosening the lock nut on Rod, and screwing up the lower nut to distance required. **Replace lock nut** when adjusted.

Oil Holes to Road Springs and Shackles should be oiled before using the Car.

Hub Caps on Front Road Wheels only, and Grease Cups on Front Axle and Steering Box, should be kept full.

The Radiator should be kept full of water.

Clutch.

Special caution should be used in the lubrication of the Clutch. **When the Car is New**, the clutch should be well oiled every day. The correct way to do this is to set the Engine running, hold out the Clutch, and let the oil run in between the Fibre and the Clutch Cone.

Should this be neglected, the Clutch will become fierce, and sieze.

Should the Clutch be neglected and seize, to release it, press Clutch Pedal, and tap all round the male part of Clutch (with Fibre on) with the shaft-end of a hammer, this will speedily release it. Then lubricate well, as described above.

6

Gear Box—
Changing of Gears.

Before changing Gears from neutral to 1st and 2nd, and from 2nd to top speeds, the Clutch Pedal should be **pressed well down** to Clutch Stop, and almost at the same time the Change-speed Lever should be pulled back to the position required.

When changing gears from top to 2nd, and from 2nd to 1st and neutral, the Clutch Pedal should **only be slightly pressed down**, sufficient to ease the Clutch.

It is advisable, when stopping the Car, **not to move the Gear Lever** to the neutral position until the Car is stationary, otherwise an unnecessarily heavy strain is put on the gears.

Should the Engine or Gear Box be taken down, or to pieces for any cause, on no account must the **bottom half of either Crank Case or Gear Box** be moved or loosened.

Neglect of the above instructions will cause breakage of the corners of the gear teeth, for which we shall not be responsible.

Clutch Stop.

This should be kept adjusted to **allow a quarter-of-an-inch** movement of the Clutch, to ensure easy changing of gear.

Lubrication of Gear Box.

This should be kept three-quarters full of either a soft Vasoleum Grease or an extra heavy Gear Oil. Inspection may be made from the lid of the Gear Box, and should be done every 400 to 500 miles.

7

The "NEW PICK" LIGHT CAR

14 to 16 h.p. (R.A.C. Rating 20-h.p.)
4 Cylinders.

PRICE - 170 Guineas.
With high-tension Magneto

Manufactured by

The New Pick Motor Company, Stamford

J. E. C. Potter, Catalogue Printer, Stamford.

INTRODUCTION.

The NEW PICK MOTOR Co. present particulars of their 1910 Car and beg to thank their many clients for the generous support and recommendation which have been accorded them during the past nine years.

This Car is the acme of simplicity, quietness of running, and ease of control. And it is confidently asserted that there is no other Car on the market to compare with it in price and reliability.

TERMS OF BUSINESS.

PRICE, as contained herein, is NETT CASH, and subject to alteration without notice.

PAYMENT. One-third Deposit with the Order, Balance on receipt of Invoice.

DELIVERY. At our Works only.

TESTING. All Cars are thoroughly tested on the road before being painted.

FOR EXPORT ORDERS. Cars are Packed in closed cases, which are charged at NETT COST, and are not returnable.

Customers requiring the use of any of our drivers or officials to drive, instruct in driving, or to handle their car, for any purpose whatever, either in taking delivery of a new car, or making adjustments or repairs to customers' cars, must accept responsibility and take all risks, either for damage to third party, to property, or to the car in use.

All Repairs and Alterations must be paid for when completed, and before the Car or part, as the case may be, is returned to the Owner.

SPECIFICATION.

MOTOR—14-16 H.P. R.A.C. Rating 20 H.P.
Four Cylinders cast separately, Mechanically Worked Inlet
Valves, Bore 90 m/m, Stroke 103 m/m, with bearings between
each throw of Crank.

NORMAL SPEED OF ENGINE.
1,500 revolutions per minute.

GEAR BOX.
Three Speeds and Reverse. Direct drive on Top Speed.

CLUTCH.
Cone shape, lined with fabric ; guaranteed to be one of the
best clutches known.

CARDEN DRIVE.
From Gear Box to back Axle, cased in with one Universal
joint near Gear Box.

BACK AXLE.
Live Axle, treble row ball bearings, hardened steel bevelled
wheels, differential spur gear type, with 3 pairs of pinions,
and expanding brakes.

WATER CIRCULATING PUMP.
Centrifugal, gear driven.

CARBURETTOR.
G. & A. with Automatic Air.

PETROL SUPPLY.
Under seat, holding 8 gallons, gravity feed.

IGNITION.
High-tension Magneto.

ARTILLERY WHEELS.
Dunlop Tyres, 800 × 80 m/m to Two-seated Car.
    ,,   800 × 85 m/m to Four-seated Car.
    ,,   810 × 90 m/m £5 extra to Four-seated Car.

WHEEL BASE.
9 feet.

FRAME.
Pressed Steel, with bottom cased in, Push Pedals to Clutch,
Foot Brake and Accelerator.

STANDARD BODY.
Two-seated or Four-seated as illustrated, finished in Napier
Green, suitably lined and trimmed.

WEIGHTS.
Thirteen and Fourteen cwt. respectively.

LUBRICATION.
Force feed.

Price	-	-	£170 Guineas	Two-Seated with High-tension Magneto
,,	-	-	£190 ,,	Four-Seated ,, ,,

3

The "New Pick," 1910.

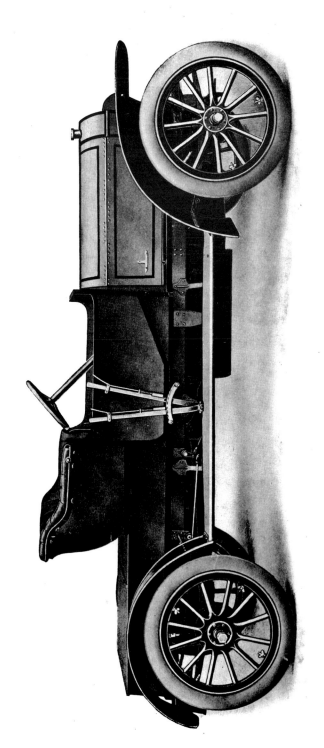

Price - 170 Guineas.

With High-tension Magneto

14-16 H.P. 4 Cylinders (R.A.C. Rating 20 H.P.)

The "New Pick," 1910.

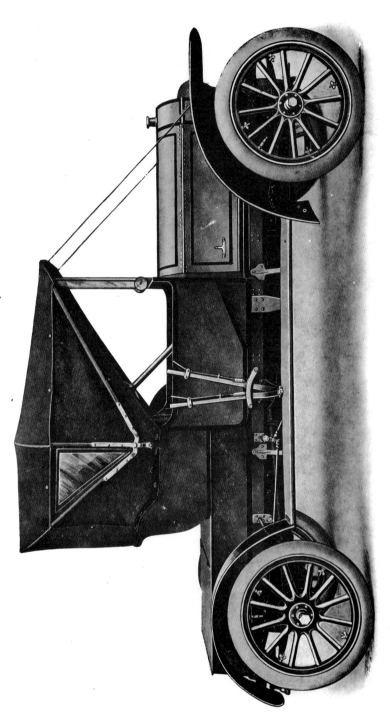

Price - 170 Guineas.

With Hood and Screen as illustrated £16 extra.

With High-tension Magneto.

14-16 H.P. 4 Cylinders (R.A.C. Rating 20 H.P.)

The "New Pick," 1910.

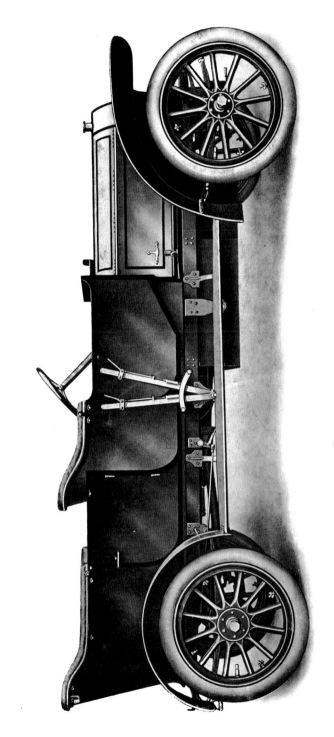

Price - 195 Guineas

With High-tension Magneto

14-16 H.P. 4 Cylinders (R.A.C. Rating 20H.P.)

The "New Pick," 1910.

Price - 195 Guineas.

With Hood and Screen £22 extra.
With High-tension Magneto.

14-16 H.P. 4 Cylinders (R.A.C. Rating 20 H.P.)

The 'New Pick' 1910 Racer.

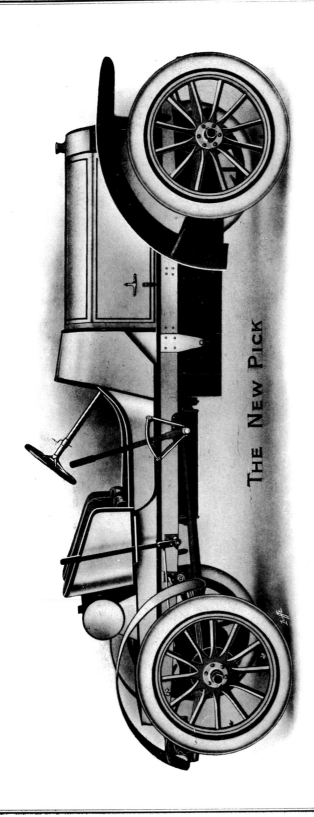

THE NEW PICK

Price - 170 Guineas.

With High-tension Magneto.

14-16 H.P. 4 Cylinders (R.A.C. Rating 20 H.P.)

Well capable of 50 miles per hour.

The "New Pick" 1910 Semi-Racer.

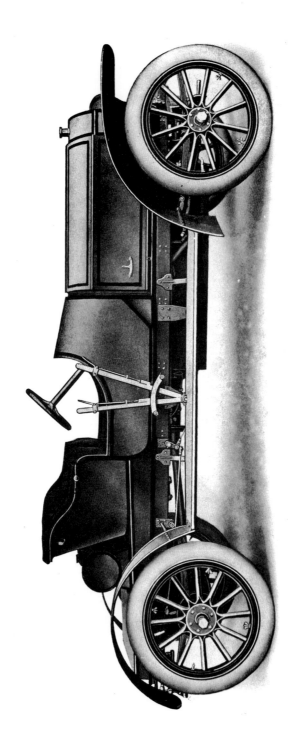

Price - 175 Guineas

With High-tension Magneto.

14-16 H.P. 4 Cylinders (R.A.C. Rating 20 H.P.)

The "New Pick," 1910 Engine.

Inlet side, shewing Magneto and Carburettor.

14-16 H.P. (R.A.C. Rating 20 H.P.)

The "New Pick," 1910 Chassis.

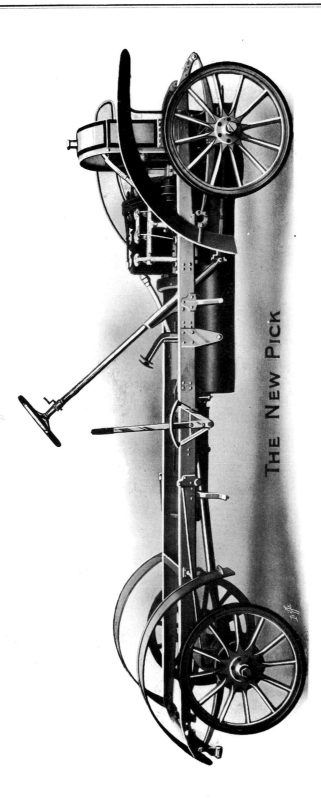

THE NEW PICK

Price, Chassis only - 144 Guineas

As illustrated, but with Bonnet.

14-16 H.P. (R.A.C. Rating 20 H.P.)

11

Motor Parts.

Price List of the various parts of the "New Pick" Motor.

Any part despatched immediately on receipt of cash.

No.			£	s.	d.
1	Inlet or exhaust valve and spring complete	each	0	7	0
2	Piston gudgeon pin, in case hardened steel	"	0	1	6
3	Valve tappet, case hardened steel	"	0	1	6
4	Exhaust or inlet cam	"	0	4	0
5	Tappet guide, bronze	"	0	3	0
6	End crank, bronze bearings	per pair	0	5	3
7	Centre bearings, bronze	"	0	4	0
8	Half time shaft bearing	each	0	2	6
9	Half time flange, eccentric bearing	"	0	4	3
10	Half time shaft, centre bearing	"	0	2	9
11	Piston Ring	"	0	0	8
12	Centre bearing cap	"	0	1	9
13	Brass pump gear wheel	"	0	6	0
14	Petrol tap. complete	"	0	0	9
15	Sparking Plug	each	0	2	6
16	Crank nut	"	0	0	9
17	Screwed plug	"	0	3	0
18	Fan spindle	"	0	2	3
19	Ball-bearing disc for fan	"	0	0	8
20	Crank box relief valve	"	0	2	6
21	Ball thrust washer	per pair	0	2	0
22	Copper and asbestos washers for screwed plugs, each		0	0	4
23	Hot air union and linings, complete	"	0	0	10
24	Water unions	"	0	0	8
25	Water lining	"	0	0	8
26	Grease stopper for pump	"	0	1	9
27	Starting clutch for crank	"	0	1	6
28	Connecting rod, complete	"	0	16	6
29	Timing gear wheel	"	0	10	6
30	Main shaft timing gear wheel	"	0	8	6
31	Magneto Wheel	"	0	8	6
32	Fan Pulley	"	0	5	0
33	Piston	"	0	11	6
34	Water pump	"	0	4	6
35	Oil pump glass	"	0	1	6
36	Oil pump, complete	"	0	9	6
37	Special connecting rod stud	"	0	0	6
38	Water pump spindle	"	0	3	6
39	Water pump paddle	"	0	4	6
40	Half timing cam spindle	"	0	2	6
41	4-throw crank, as illustrated	"	6	15	0
42	Sparking plug spanner	"	0	1	6
43	Water circulating pump complete	"	1	10	0
44	Cylinder, as illustrated	"	3	10	0
45	Magneto complete, less pinion	"	9	15	0

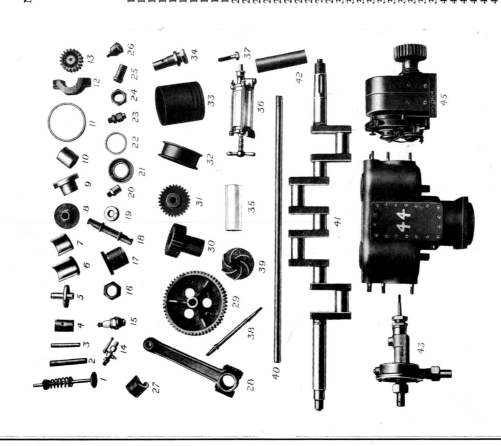

Gear Box Parts.

Price List of the various parts of the "New Pick" Motor.

Any part despatched immediately on receipt of cash.

No.	Part		£	s.	d.
46	3-speed sleeve	...	3	12	0
47	Reverse wheel	...	1	5	0
48	Toggle gear sleeve	per pair	1	7	6
49	Sliding gear sleeve	...	2	10	6
50	Gear box countershaft, case hardened steel	...	0	7	6
51	Clutch spindle	...	0	3	0
52	Reverse spindle, case hardened steel	...	0	1	6
53	Main gear box shaft	...	1	0	0
54	Main gear box bearings	per pair	0	10	0
55	Main groove bearing	,,	0	12	0
56	Sliding rod fork	...	0	1	9
57	Cardan drive crosshead	...	0	4	0
58	Cardan crosshead bolt, case hardened steel	...	0	1	2
59	Gear box striking fork	...	0	2	3
60	Foot brake part	...	0	1	3
61	Foot brake part	...	0	0	9
62	Cardan drive fork	...	0	4	9
63	Foot brake link	...	0	1	6
64	Ball race holder for clutch	...	0	0	8
65	Ball race for clutch	...	0	2	0
66	Clutch pedal fork	...	0	4	6
67	Clutch spring	...	0	2	6
68	Foot brake drum	...	0	9	0
69	Half foot brake band	...	0	4	0
70	Second half brake band	...	0	3	9
71	Foot pedal	each	0	3	6
72	Carburettor	...	3	17	6
73	Clutch stop	...	0	3	0
74	Joint	each	0	0	8
75	Joint	,,	0	0	8
76	Clutch fibre	...	0	4	6

13

Back and Front Axle Parts, etc.

Price List of the various parts of the "New Pick" Motor.

Any part despatched immediately on receipt of cash.

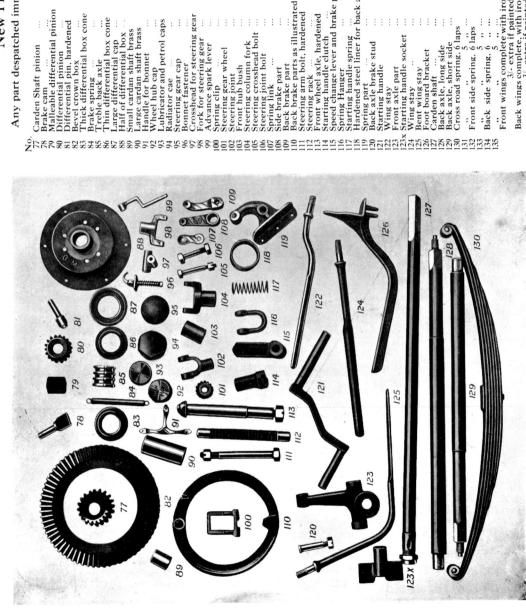

No.			£	s.	d.
77	Carden Shaft pinion		1	6	3
78	Brake cam		0	1	8
79	Malleable differential pinion	each	0	6	0
80	Differential pinion		0	12	0
81	Differential pin, hardened		0	1	0
82	Bevel crown box		3	15	0
83	Thick differential box cone		0	3	6
84	Brake spring		0	0	6
85	Treble back axle		0	10	6
86	Thin differential box cone		0	8	6
87	Large differential cap		0	1	6
88	Half of differential box		0	9	6
89	Small cardan shaft brass		0	11	6
90	Large cardan shaft brass		0	3	6
91	Handle for bonnet	each	0	6	0
92	Wheel hub cap		0	2	9
93	Lubricator and petrol caps	each	0	1	6
94	Radiator cae		0	1	9
95	Steering gear cap		0	1	6
96	Bonnet fastener		0	2	3
97	Crosshead for steering gear		0	3	6
98	Fork for steering gear		0	10	8
99	Advance spark lever		0	3	6
100	Spring clip		0	0	8
101	Steering gear wheel		0	3	8
102	Steering joint		0	3	0
103	Front hub bush		0	2	0
104	Steering column fork		0	2	9
105	Steering crosshead bolt		0	1	6
106	Steering joint bolt		0	1	6
107	Spring link		0	1	6
108	Side brake part		0	0	8
109	Back brake part		0	5	6
110	Back brake parts as illustrated		0	15	0
111	Steering arm bolt, hardened		0	1	6
112	Steering rack		0	6	6
113	Front wheel axle, hardened	each	0	8	5
114	Starting handle clutch		0	5	6
115	Speed change lever and brake part		0	2	6
116	Spring Hanger		0	1	0
117	Starting handle spring	each	0	0	6
118	Hardened steel liner for back axle		0	2	8
119	Spring part		0	2	3
120	Back axle brake stud		0	2	6
121	Starting handle		0	2	0
122	Wing stay		0	1	6
123	Front axle part		2	4	0
123x	Starting handle socket		0	10	0
124	Bent wing stay		0	1	6
125	Wing stay		0	2	6
126	Foot board bracket		0	9	6
127	Carden shaft		0	8	6
128	Back axle, long side		0	8	6
129	Back axle, short side		0	7	6
130	Cross road spring, 6 laps		0	7	6
131	Front side spring, 5		0	7	6
132	Front side spring, 6 laps		0	7	6
133	Back side spring, 5 "		0	7	6
134	Back side "spring, 6 "		0	7	6
135	" " "		0	12	0
	Front wings complete with irons, painted lead colour		0	12	0
	3/- extra if painted in colour				
	Back wings complete, with irons painted lead colour		0	12	0
	3/- extra if painted in colour				

14

Compare the following advantages in this Car over other Cars offered at the same price.

CHASSIS—Pressed Steel.

CARBURETTOR—G. & A., with Automatic Air.

CLUTCH—Cone Shape, lined with Fabric; equal to any metal Clutch.

CAR AND ENGINE—Smooth and quiet running; handles as easily as the most expensive Car.

ENGINE—Four Cylinder; up-to-date in every respect; 14-16 h.p.

FAN—Drive with flat belt. Ball Bearings.

HIGH TENSION MAGNETO

MOTOR BEARINGS—Five to Crank Shaft.

PUMP—Gear Driven.

PETROL CONSUmPTION—Twenty-eight miles to the gallon.

SPEED—Average, 30 miles per hour; will climb long hills of 1 in 9 on top speed.

WHEEL BASE—Eight and nine feet respectively.

WHEELS—Thirty-two inch.

WEIGHT. Thirteen and fourteen cwt. respectively. Light on Tyres.

Engine, Gear Box, Carburettor, Pump, Magneto, all easy of access.

OUTSIDE MEASUREMENTS of "New Pick" Cars—12ft. long, 5ft. wide.

SIZE OF CASES for shipment—12ft. × 5ft. × 5ft.

Nota Bene.—Notice Illustration of Motor and Side-View of Car.
Notice it has the same features as a large expensive Car.
You will not find like advantages in any other Car sold at the same price.
All parts are interchangeable. See Price List.

Price of strong Water-tight Crate and Packing for Shipment .... £7 10s. nett.

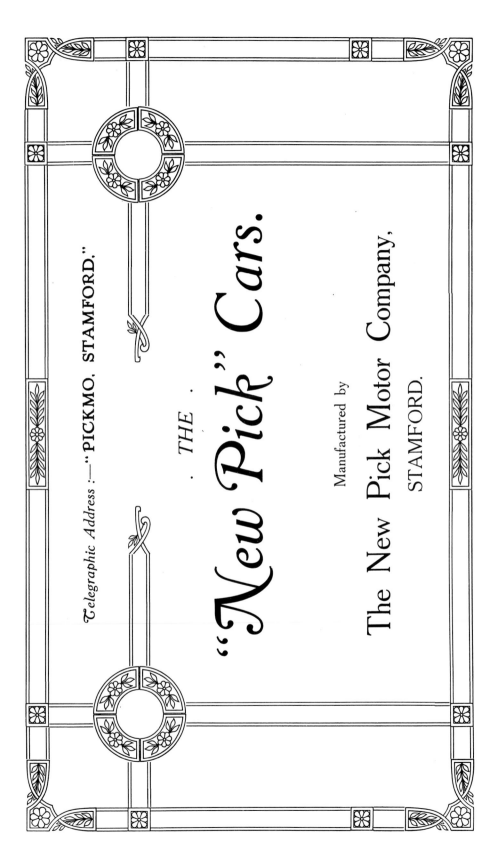

Telegraphic Address :—"PICKMO, STAMFORD."

. THE .

"New Pick" Cars.

Manufactured by

The New Pick Motor Company,

STAMFORD.

INTRODUCTION.

THE NEW PICK MOTOR Co. present particulars of their Cars and beg to thank their many clients for the generous support and recommendation which have been accorded them during the past eleven years.

This Car is the acme of simplicity, quietness of running, and ease of control. And it is confidently asserted that there is no other Car on the market to compare with it in price and reliability.

TERMS OF BUSINESS.

PRICE, as contained herein, is NETT CASH, and subject to alteration without notice.

PAYMENT. One-third Deposit with the Order, Balance on receipt of Invoice.

DELIVERY. At our Works only.

TESTING. All Cars are thoroughly tested on the road before being painted.

FOR EXPORT ORDERS. Cars are Packed in closed cases, which are charged at NETT COST, and are not returnable.

Customers requiring the use of any of our drivers or officials to drive, instruct in driving, or to handle their car, for any purpose whatever, either in taking delivery of a new car, or making adjustments or repairs to customers' cars, must accept responsibility and take all risks, either for damage to third party, to property, or to the car in use.

All Repairs and Alterations must be paid for when completed, and before the Car or part, as the case may be, is returned to the Owner.

When it comes to the selection of a Motor Car,

Simplicity, Comfort and Economy are the chief essentials to consider.

Let your choice be THE NEW PICK, the 'All-British Car, made at Stamford, Lincoln.

——— THERE'S A REASON ! READ ON. ———

THE CAR FOR THE MODERATE MAN.

THE NEW PICK CAR places really luxurious Motoring within the reach of all men of moderate means. First, because the

Small Initial Outlay. initial outlay is comparatively small, and, lastly, for the big reason that the cost of maintenance is only a trifle more than Third Class Railway travelling.

The man who needs a Motor Car for business or pleasure will at once appreciate the many advantages the "New Pick" offers, for apart from its economy,

Driving Easily Mastered. it is so simple, so easily controlled and so dependably made, that the veriest tyro can quickly master the details of its construction—a point that will appeal to all those who intend to drive the car themselves.

Take control for instance. Nothing can possibly get out of order. Changing gears is quite an easy matter—not the slightest judgment being required,—and the foot levers, speed changes and clutch are manipulated by movements which cannot be misunderstood.

3

If the practical man of business, who is wanting a Motor Car, will make a thorough investigation of the "New Pick," he will at once admit its great superiority. and it goes without saying that the more you know of it, the better you will appreciate it.

THE "NEW PICK" CAR is the result of exhaustive experiments by experienced Motor Engineers, who have had in view the whole while a

Complication Eliminated. fixed desire to eliminate all complication, and to substitute labour and money-saving devices, which is not merely good designing, but rather good sense.

The Clutch is so perfectly balanced, that whilst it can be disengaged by the slightest pressure of the foot, yet it never slips.

Noiseless Gear Changing. The gear pinions slide easily, change without burring, and operate noiselessly,

and the whole Car is a delight to an expert and a pleasure to the novice.

Now it is not wise to depend too much on the recommendation of others when selecting a Motor Car. A friend will naturally try to justify his own selection. A Chauffeur may be prejudiced, or lack experience, and the dealer has, of course, his own axe to grind.

Your own opinion, after a trial, is far the best guide, although there are naturally one or **Test it for Yourself.** two matters on which the honest dealer's opinion will prove helpful, for it frequently happens that the buyer of a Car is led away by the skilful salesman, who glosses over any imperfection by directing the buyer's attention to superfluous fitments which have no real bearing on the worth of the Car.

You get value for every penny invested in the "New Pick" Car, and this is why you should see it before deciding on another make.

SPECIFICATIONS.

Frame. Pressed Steel of " U " Section.

Wheel Base. Nine feet.

Tread. Four feet.

Springs. Semi-elliptic, with transverse rear spring.

Wheels. Artillery pattern.

Cylinders, 4 Cylinders cast in one piece, having a bore of 90 m.m. and a stroke of 127 m.m.

Horse Power. 16-18 (R.A.C. Rating 22 h.p.)

Carburetter. Zenith.

Ignition. Simms' high tension magneto.

Valves. Inlet and exhaust valves are at the same side, and enclosed by two plates which can be removed by undoing four screws.

Induction and Exhaust. These pipes are a single casting, which assures a particularly clean design of engine.

Lubrication. Semi-splash feed to big ends, assisted by pressure from auxiliary tank.

Water Circulation. Thermo-Syphon principle, with pipes of extra large diameter to assure a perfectly even circulation under all conditions. The cooling is assisted by a fan on ball bearings.

Clutch. The gentlest clutch made. Red fibre segments engaging with a metal cone. It never slips nor engages fiercely.

Gears. Three speeds forward and reverse, of the sliding pinion type, beautifully smooth engagement at any speed.

Transmission. By Cardan shaft running on ball bearings, and enclosed in a perfectly dust-proof case.

Back Axle. Bevel wheel and pinion, ball bearings throughout.

Steering. Worm and Sector.

Brakes. Foot pedal brake, external expanding type. Shoes lined with composition. Side hand brake, internal expanding.

Control. By foot acceleration operating the throttle valve.

PRICE— **Standard Two-Seater, fitted 800 by 80 Tyres.**

PRICE— **Standard Four-Seater, fitted 800 by 85 Tyres.**

The Motor fitted to The "New Pick" Cars.

Near Side View of Motor
showing half of Valve
Casing removed.

Also showing the fixing
of Simm's Magneto and
Zenith Carburettor.

4 Cylinder.

16-18 H.P.

$3\frac{1}{2}$ Bore, 5 in. Stroke.

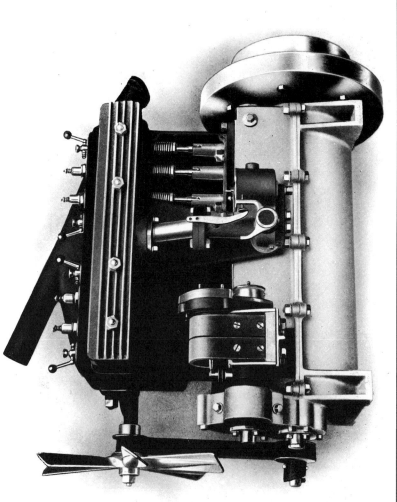

The "New Pick."

Off Side View of Motor.

———

A few Points regarding Engine

Starts first pull up of handle.

Pulls at extremely low revolutions on hills, and it is impossible to make the Engine knock.

Pistons and Cylinders never Carbon up to cause automatic firing.

The above points you seldom obtain even on a more expensive Car.

———

4 Cylinders.

16-18 H.P., $3\frac{1}{2}$ Bore, 5" Stroke.

Showing Thermo-Syphon Circulation.

7

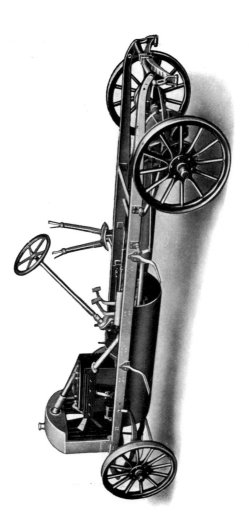

The "New Pick" Standard Chassis.

The "New Pick" Standard Two-Seater.

16-18 H.P. (R.A.C. Rating 22 H.P.)

Price   -   -

AS ILLUSTRATED.

With 800 by 80 Tyres.

Fitted with Hood and Screen, as illustrated on page 14,   extra.

If Hood not required, extra charge of   will be made for Brackets.

The "New Pick" Standard Four-Seater.

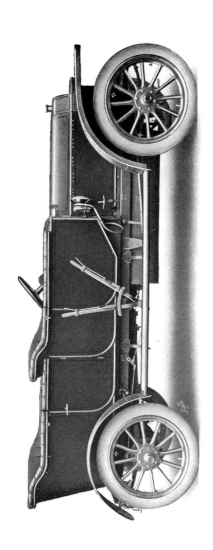

16-18 H.P. (R.A.C. Rating 22 H.P.)

Price   -   -

AS ILLUSTRATED.

With 800 by 85 Tyres.   Hood and Screen   extra.

If Hood not required, extra charge of   will be made for Brackets.

Price of British Accessories fitted to Car.

					£	s.	d.
Head Lamp	...	...	...	each			
Side Lamps	...	...	...	pair			
Tail Lamp	...	...	...	each			
Motor Horn with Tube	...	...	...				
Tool Kit	...	...	...	...			
Jack	...	...	...	...			
Pump	...	...	...	...			
Stewart Speedometer	...	...	...				
Stepney Wheel only with Fittings	...	...					
Tyre and Tube extra.							
Number Plates, lettered and fitted	...	...	pair				

If customers supply their own Accessories, fitting same will be an extra charge.

The "New Pick"
Torpedo Two and Four-Seater Cars.

FRONT VIEW

Showing Special Radiator and Bonnet.

Scuttle Dash containing large Petrol and Lubricating Tanks.

Front Axle and Flanged Mudguards.

All Levers inside body.

12

The "New Pick" Torpedo Two-Seater.

SIDE VIEW.

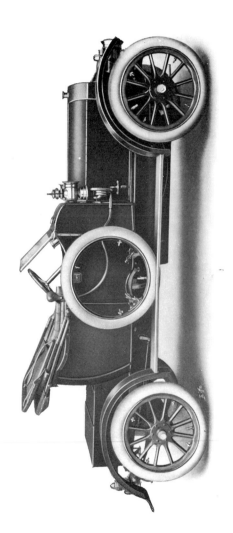

16-18 H.P. (R.A.C. Rating 22 H.P.)

With 800 by 85 Tyres, Plain.

Price   -   without Accessories.

The "New Pick" Torpedo Two-Seater.

Showing Hood up and Dicky Seat (folding).

16-18 H.P. (R.A.C. Rating 22 H.P.)

Torpedo 2-Seater, fitted with 800 by 85 plain Tyres,

			£	s.	d.
Hood and Screen	...	...	...	...	
Set of 4 Lamps	...	...	...	...	
Motor Horn with Tube	...	...	...		
Tool Kit ...	...	...	...	...	
Jack ...	...	...	...	...	
Pump ...	...	...	...	...	
Stewart Speedometer	...	...	...		
Stepney Wheel fitted with Tyre and Tube and fitted complete	...				
Number Plates, lettered and fitted	...	...			
Extra for Dicky Seat (folding)	...	...	...		
If filled in between Footboards and Body with Patent Leather on both sides					
of Chassis ...	...	...	...	...	

If customers supply their own Accessories, fitting same will be an extra charge.

If Hood not required extra charge of   will be made for Brackets.

15

The "New Pick" Torpedo Four-Seater.

See page 12 for Front View and other Particulars.

16-18 H.P. (R.A.C. Rating 22 H.P.)

Fitted with 800 by 85 Tyres, Plain.

Price   -   without Accessories.

Torpedo 4-Seater, fitted with 800 by 85 Tyres,

	£	s.	d.
Hood and Screen			
Set of 4 Lamps			
Motor Horn with Tube			
Tool Kit			
Jack			
Pump			
Stewart Speedometer			
Stepney Wheel fitted with Cover and Tube and fitted complete ...			
Number Plates, lettered and fitted			
If filled in between Footboards and Body with Patent Leather on both sides of Chassis			
If Car fitted with 810 by 90 plain Tyres instead of 800 by 85			
Stepney Wheel, fitted 810 by 90 plain, extra			

If customers supply their own Accessories, fitting same will be an extra charge.

If Hood not required extra charge of   will be made for Brackets.

The "New Pick" Heavy Landaulette, Taxi or Van Chassis.

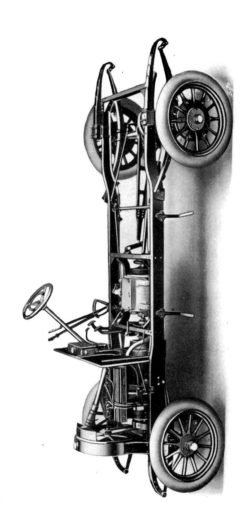

For Particulars see Pages 21 and 22.

The "New Pick" Landaulette or Taxi.

THREE-QUARTER FRONT VIEW
OF LANDAULETTE.

16-18 H.P.

(R.A.C. Rating 22 H.P.)

Price - -

Complete with Accessories.

_____

Specification on Page 21.

The "New Pick" Landaulette or Taxi.

16-18 H.P. (R.A.C. Rating 22 H.P.)

Price - - complete with Accessories.

See Specification, Page 21.

SPECIFICATION OF "NEW PICK" LANDAULETTE.

9 feet Wheel Base, 4ft. 6in. Track.

With 765 by 105 Tyres, Stepney Wheel and Tyre, 2 large Acetelyne Head Lamps, 2 Side Lamps, 1 Tail Lamp, Number Plates lettered and finished, Tool Kit, Jack, Pump, Horn, Speedometer, Clock, Oil Tin, Tyre Levers, etc.

Body splendidly finished in any colour desired. Inside to seat three, most comfortably upholstered in cloth, finished in very best style, with Arm Rests.

Speaking Trumpet to Driver, and Electric Light.

Driver's Seat, etc., trimmed with leather.

The above Car complete for

"New Pick" 10 to 15 cwt. Delivery Van.

16-18 H.P. (R.A.C. Rating 22 H.P.)   Fitted with large Solid Rubber Tyres.

Price   -   Lamps and Tools complete.

LETTERING EXTRA.

Compare the following advantages in this Car over other Cars offered at the same price.

CHASSIS—Pressed Steel.

CARBURETTOR—"Zenith."

CLUTCH—Cone Shape, lined with Fabric ; equal to any metal Clutch.

CAR AND ENGINE—Smooth and quiet running; handles as easily as the most expensive Car.

ENGINE—Four Cylinder ; up-to-date in every respect ; 16-18 h.p.

FAN—Drive with flat belt.   Ball Bearings.

HIGH TENSION MAGNETO.

MOTOR BEARINGS.

PETROL CONSUMPTION—Twenty-five miles to the gallon.

SPEED—Average, 30 miles per hour ; will climb long hills of 1 in 9 on top speed.

WHEEL BASE—Nine feet.

WEIGHT—Fifteen cwt. respectively.   Light on Tyres.

Engine, Gear Box, Carburettor, Magneto, all easy of access.

OUTSIDE MEASUREMENTS of "New Pick" Cars—12ft. long, 5ft. wide.

SIZES OF CASES for Shipment—12ft. by 5ft. by 5ft.

Nota Bene.—Notice Illustration of Motor and Side View of Car.

Notice it has the same features as a large expensive Car.

You will not find like advantages in any other Car sold at the same price.

All parts are interchangeable.   See Price List.

Price of strong Water-tight Crate and Packing for Shipment   -

A few recent remarks regarding the "New Pick" Cars.

COPY OF AN AGENT'S LETTER TO A CLIENT.

March 21st, 1911.

DEAR SIR,—With reference to your kind enquiry of the "New Pick" Motor Company, I have pleasure in enclosing latest Catalogue, and should be very pleased to give you a trial of this car. I have a chassis on view, and should be very glad if you would call and inspect it, as I think you will be more than interested in the clever and mechanical manner in which this car is made. In the matter of price it compares with the cheap and nasty American cars, with their old-fashioned epicyclic gears, cheap American tyres, old-fashioned tall chassis, and bodywork that is ten years behind the times. The "New Pick" can of course be fitted with any body, and at the price is the most wonderful value in the market. Moreover, it is an English car, made by an old-established Firm, and will always fetch a good price second-hand. The particular pattern I have will take practically every hill in the district on top speed, and I should very much like to give you a trial.

GOODWIN.

February, 1911.

DEAR SIR,—I want to give my husband a mascot for his car, and want to get a Lincoln Imp in brass. Do you know a Lincoln Firm likely to keep them, or, better still, do you keep them? The car is a flyer; no need for a flying machine now.

(MRS.) N. TISDALL JOHNS.

March 17th, 1911.

DEAR SIR,—The car you supplied me with about a month ago runs beautifully. I am quite satisfied with her.

Yours faithfully, LESLIE POYSON.

March 25th, 1911.

DEAR SIR,—Having run one of your cars for four seasons on Irish and Welsh roads, doing from eighty to ninety thousand miles on the roughest of roads, I have decided to have one of your new models." Please put same in hand, and let me know how soon you can deliver.

Yours truly, F. PRICE.

April 17th, 1911.

DEAR SIR,—I may add up to this the car has been running splendidly and given no trouble whatever. I consider you cars are very good value for money.—I remain,

Dear Sirs, Yours faithfully, F. HILLYARD.

March 19th, 1911.

DEAR SIR,—Please put in hand for me one of your new model cars and deliver as soon as possible. I sold my "Pick" car yesterday for £100 to a dealer after running same for three seasons.

Faithfully yours, GEO. MUTTER.

May 8th, 1911.

DEAR SIR,—I have now had the car two years, and have done well over 20,000 miles. It has given me every satisfaction, and is running now as well as ever. I did 112 miles run last week on four gallons of petrol (twenty-eight miles to the gallon). There are very few four-cylinder cars in this neighbourhood that can at any time do more than twenty-five miles to the gallon.

I am, yours faithfully, Dr. D. R. PRICE.

June 26th, 1911.

DEAR SIR,—My husband wishes me to say he has sent off to-day a mudguard. Will you kindly have it straightened out and re-painted, and return as soon as possible. We drove her to Bristol on Saturday, and her powers of going across country as well as on the road we tested well, as my husband had to take a two-foot curb grip to avoid a cart that had backed across the road, but so far we can find no damage, although I am sure most cars would have gone to matchwood in the test. I believe she has run 4,000 miles now, and at last I am bound to think a car can be built in England for an American price.

Truly yours, (MRS.) N. TISDALL JOHNS.

The PICK Saloon.

Manufactured by THE PICK MOTOR Co. Ltd., STAMFORD.

INTRODUCTORY.

THE " PICK " CAR is no novelty. The first car was, in point of fact, manufactured some 25 years ago, and was exhibited at the Stanley Cycle Show at the Agricultural Hall, long before the days of Motor Exhibitions at Crystal Palace or Olympia.

Since then the Car has forged its way to the very front rank through sheer merit, and entirely unaided by advertisement, until to-day it has a considerable and ever-increasing circle of staunch admirers.

The explanation of its success is not far to seek, and forms the keynote of the numerous testimonials received by the Company. Put in a few words, its success is due to the extraordinary reliability, durability, efficiency and economical running of the car.

IT IS BRITISH MADE THROUGHOUT, and follows recognised British lines, both in the substantial design and construction of the mechanism, and the solid comfort and essentially English appearance.

The present model is the final outcome of 25 years' experience, and is a typical example of the wonderful results to be obtained (both as regards *perfection* and *cheapness* of manufacture), by specialisation and concentration on one definite object; the ultimate result in the present case being a car with practically every up-to-date refinement, *absolutely complete and ready for the road*, which will be found the equal of any car within £100 of the extremely moderate price asked.

In ordering a " PICK " CAR, therefore, the purchaser will not only be making a sound investment which will afford him complete and permanent satisfaction, but he will be materially encouraging and assisting British enterprise and British workmen.

The 1924 Four Seater (22·5 h.p.)

Price - £385

EQUIPMENT :

Smith's or Lucas' Self-Starter and Dynamo.

Head, Side, Tail Lamps and Electric Horn.

Aluminium Instrument Board,
beautifully finished and fully equipped with Clock and Speedometer.

Bluemel's 18in. Steering Wheel

5 Wheels fitted with 765×105 Best Dunlop Cord Tyres.

A Full Equipment of Tools with Enots Grease Gun.

Length—10 ft.   Wheel Base—4 ft. 7 in.   Track—13 ft. 8 in. over all.

THE COACH WORK.—Four Seater Sports Model Body is designed on novel and comfortable lines, with strength; the seating being low, guarantees the passengers being protected from wind and weather by the scuttle dash, the skeleton is made of prime English ash, the panels are heavy gauge aluminium, which ensures no rusting to raise the paint—also lightness.

The "PICK" Patent Perfect Seats are fitted to this body, these are all moveable, and can be taken out in five minutes, for sleeping accommodation, or carrying luggage, the driving seat being adjustable to suit any driver, *these features should not be overlooked.*

Upholstering of the best quality and finish, with a neat one man hood, notice the height of the footboards and shape of mudguards ; saving ground friction means increased speed, less Petrol consumption with less dust, splashes, and suction on car.

The PICK Sporting Model

The 1924 Sporting Model (22.5 h.p.)

Price - £365

EQUIPMENT:

Smith's or Lucas' Self-Starter and Dynamo.

Head, Side, Tail Lamps and Electric Horn.

Aluminium Instrument Board,

beautifully finished and fully equipped with Smith's Clock and Speedometer.

Bluemel's 18in. Steering Wheel.

5 Wheels (fitted with 765×105 Best Dunlop Cord Tyres.)

A Full Equipment of Tools with Enots Grease Gun.

Length—10 ft.   Wheel Base—4 ft. 7 in.   Track—13 ft. 8 in. over all.

THE COACH WORK.—Two Seater Sports Model Body is designed on novel and comfortable lines; with strength; the seating being low guarantees the passengers being protected from wind and weather by the scuttle dash. The skeleton is made of prime seasoned English ash, the panels are heavy gauge aluminium, which guarantees no rusting to raise the paint, also lightness, a feature that should not be *overlooked*. **Upholstering** of the best quality and finish, with a neat one man hood. Notice the shape of the mudguards and height of foot boards ; saving ground friction means increased speed, less Petrol consumption, with less dust, splashes, and suction on car.

The PICK Four-Seater Sports Model or Touring Car

The Reason Why YOU Should Buy a "PICK" 22·5 h.p., in Preference to a 10 h.p. Car ——

1. YOU get A **High=grade Car.**

2. YOU get your one **Choice of Colour or Polished Aluminium.**

3. YOU get **Thirty Miles** to the **Gallon of Petrol.**

4. YOU get **Sixty Miles per Hour Speed if required.**

5. YOU get **Large Tyres** and **Long Wheel Base**—these guarantee smooth running on rough roads.

6. YOU get no engine whirl as you are doing over **Forty Miles** per hour at a 1,000 revolutions as against 3,000 on a 10 h.p., which means three times the wear and tear.

7. YOU get **Three Times the Value** in the equipment.

8. YOU get a **Car** in **Appearance** together with **Comfort** and a **Pleasure** to drive.

9. YOU get a **Car** that is **Easy to Drive in Traffic on Top Gear**—very slow.

10. YOU get a **Car** which is unpassable for speed at anything like the price.

11. YOU get a **Car** that is **Worth Twice as much after Three Years Wear** as a 10 h.p. Car.

The 1924 Coupe (22·5 h.p.)

Price - £410

EQUIPMENT :

Smith's or Lucas' Self-Starter and Dynamo.

Head, Side, Tail Lamps and Electric Horn.

Aluminium Instrument Board, beautifully finished and fully equipped with Clock and Speedometer

5 Wheels fitted with 765 × 105 Dunlop Best Cord Tyres.

Bluemel's 18 in. Steering Wheel.

A Full Equipment of Tools with Enots Grease Gun.

Length—10 ft.   Wheel Base—4 ft. 7 in.   Track—13 ft. 8 in. over all.

The COUPE Coach Work is designed with a V front for less wind resistance, and V back to avoid suction, the skeleton is made of prime English ash, Window Fittings, etc., are all nickel-plated, the panels being heavy gauge aluminium, which ensures no rusting to raise paint—also lightness.

The "PICK" Patent Perfect Seats are used, these being adjustable and moveable, all the above items should not be *overlooked*.

The Upholstering is of the highest possible grade, Bedford Cord being used for the seats and bottom quarters, the roof and top quarters being finished in smooth cloth, with lace and curtains to match.

All Parts manufactured by us.

The "PICK" Engine opposite is Off-Side View,

Showing———

Dynamo on Rocking Base for Tightening Belt,
Accessibility of Zenith Carburettor and Oil Filler.

The Cooling-Thermo-Syphon

Below shows———

Crankshaft with Three Main Long Bearings of
big diameter, and throws in proportion, also
Camshaft with Three Long Bearings, Silent Chain
Wheel and Spiral Pump Wheel.

———

*The Main Bearings, Big End and Cam Shaft
are Phosphor Bronze Shells lined with White Metal.*

All Parts manufactured by us.

The "PICK" 4-cylinder Engine

(22·5 h.p., 95 m/m bore, 127 m/m stroke).

Is fitted to all Cars
illustrated within.

The Engine opposite, showing the near side view, with part of Tappet Case removed.

Please Note———

THE CLEAN DESIGN AND ACCESSIBILITY
OF ALL PARTS.

◆ ◆ ◆

M.L. Magneto Starter, Tappets and Sparking Plugs.
Below shows the Piston and Connecting Rod.

————————————

The Engine at 850 revolutions gives 24 h.p.
,, ,, will give up to 3,000 revolutions.

The PICK Saloon.

The 1924 Saloon (22·5 h.p.)

Price - £450

EQUIPMENT :

Smith's or Lucas' Self-Starter and Dynamo.

Head, Side, Tail, Lamps and Electric Horn.

Aluminium Instrument Board
beautifully finished and fully equipped with
Clock and Speedometer.

Bluemel's 18 in. Steering Wheel.

5 Wheels fitted with 815×120 Dunlop
Best Cord Tyres.

A Full Equipment of Tools with Enots
Grease Gun.

Length—10 ft. 10 in.   Wheel Base—4 ft. 7 in.   Track—14 ft. 8 in. over all.

The SALOON Coach Work is designed with V front and back, as illustrated, to save wind resistance and suction, the skeleton being prime Ash, the Windows being fitted with Beclawat lifts, etc., and body panelled with heavy gauge aluminium, the roof having a Ventilator and Electric Roof Light, all fittings being electro plated.

The " PICK " Patent Perfect Seats are fitted to these bodies, these being moveable, and can be taken out in five minutes for sleeping accommodation or carrying luggage, the driving seat being adjustable to suit any driver ; these features should not be *overlooked.*

The Upholstering is of the highest possible grade, Bedford Cord being used for the seats and bottom quarters, the roof and top quarters being finished in smooth cloth, with lace and curtains to match.

1　Exhaust Cam.

2　Inlet Cam.

3　Spiral Gear on Camshaft.

4　Spiral Gear on Lifting Screw.

5　Oil Lifting Screw.

6　Oil Inlet to Screw.

7　Oil Sump.

8　Oil Troughs for Big Ends.

8a　Gap for Return Oil to Sump.

9　Oil Scoops on Big Ends.

10　Oil Pipes to Main Bearings.

11　Oil Distributing Channel.

12　Valve Tappet.

13　Oil Filler.

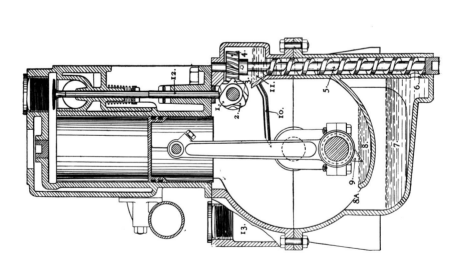

Sectional Drawing Opposite Showing a Non-Failing System for White Metal Bearings.

The system of Lubrication in the "PICK" Engine is unique. An "Archimedean screw" is employed instead of the usual pump, this being operated from the cam shaft by worm gear.

The oil is lifted by the Archimedean screw from a sump in the crank-case to a trough, and distributed therefrom to the three main bearings by pipes.

The overflow from this trough and from the pipes is collected in four lower troughs situated under the big ends, whence it is distributed to the big ends and cylinders by means of oil scoops fitted to the lower extremity of the big-end bearings, the overflow returning to the sump.

Rear View of Chassis.

Rear View of Chassis

(See Illustration Opposite).

Note —————

Large Air Cooled Brake Drums with Two Levers and Rods to each, also the Two Torque Rods from Back Axle.

The Cardan Shaft being parallel saves wear on Universal Joints.

Engine, Gear Box, Clutch and Back Axle being all separate units, are Simplicity—and Best.

THE CLUTCH (Cone Shape—Friction Fibre Lined) has proved to be one of the best in work.

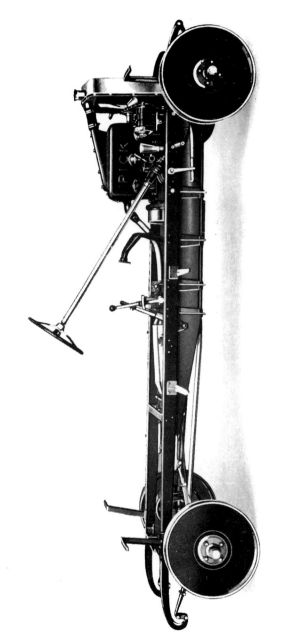

Side View of Chassis.

All Parts Manufactured by us.

Side View of Chassis.

The Chassis Side Members are of a Heavy Channel Section.

The Cross Hangers and Members that carry Engine and Gear Box are of T Section.

The Road Springs (Long, Semi-Elliptic)—Very Best Quality.

Spring Bolts, &c., are fitted with Enot's Greasers.

Cooling Thermo-Syphon fitted with "Sercks" Radiator.

5 Detachable Disc Wheel, 765×105.

The Saloon Chassis Wheels are 815×120.

The Steering Gear is of the Worm and Sector Type, all wearing parts being Stampings of "Ubas" Steel (case hardened), with Ball Thrust Washers and Phosphor Bronze Bushes.

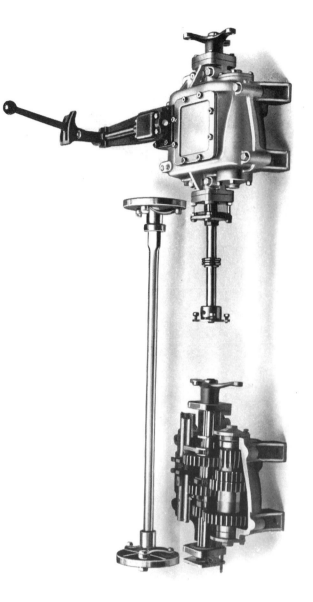

The "PICK" Heavy Gate Change Gear Box.

All Parts Manufactured by us.

The " PICK " Heavy Gate Change Gear Box.

Showing——

Cardan Shaft with Leather Discs. and

Coupling, Clutch Stop, and Shaft to Engine.

GEARS AND SHAFTS ARE ALL MADE FROM " UBAS " STEEL.

STAMPINGS ACCURATELY MACHINED,
PROPERLY HARDENED AND GROUND.

The Strength and Quality proved to be Unbreakable.

GEARS RATIO APPROXIMATE.

First Speed Engine	-	$8\frac{1}{2}$ revolutions	= Road Wheels -	1
Second ,,	,,	$4\frac{1}{4}$,,	= ,, -	1
Third ,,	,,	$2\frac{1}{8}$,,	= ,, -	1
Reverse ,,	,,	- 10 ,,	= ,, ,,	1

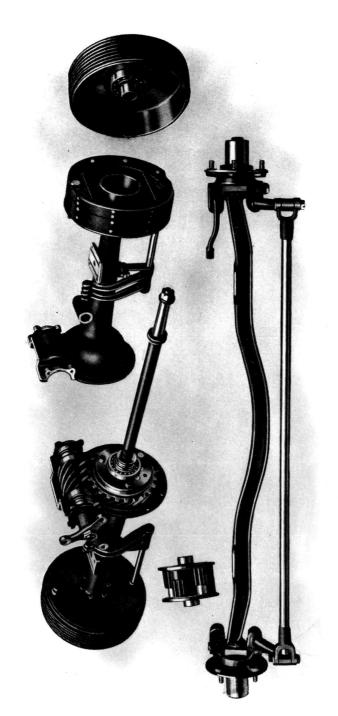

The " PICK " Back and Front Axle,

With one side of the casing removed, showing the large diameter and coarse threads of the worm that make the " PICK " Axle such a success ; also the large heavy type of Ball Bearings and Thrust Washers.

The Foot and Side Brakes are of large diameter, both operating side by side.

The Brake Covers are moveable, which saves drawing Hub when Shoes want Re-lining.

Following are the

APPROXIMATE RATIO OF WORM GEAR FITTED

SPORTING MODEL Top Worm Engine - $2\frac{1}{8}$ revolutions $=$ Road Wheels 1

FOUR SEATER ,, ,, ,, - $2\frac{1}{2}$,, $=$,, 1

COUPE ,, ,, ,, - $2\frac{1}{2}$,, $=$,, 1

PULLMAN ,, ,, ,, - $3\frac{1}{8}$,, $=$,, 1

The Front Axle is an H Section 40-ton Tensile Steel Stamping, the Swivel Heads and Arms being Stampings of the same material.

Our Brakes we claim to be second to none, as they have 216 square inches surface of genuine " Ferrodo " Lining.

At the Stanley Cycle Show—24 Years Ago.

This "**PICK**" **C**ar was manufactured and **E**xhibited by us at the **A**gricultural **H**all long before the days of **M**otor **E**xhibitions at **C**rystal **P**alace and **O**lympia,

Reprinted from " THE AUTOCAR," March 30th, 1923.

THE 22·5 h.p. SPORTING PICK.

A Fast Car with a Relatively Large and Slow-Speed Four-Cylinder Engine.

Long and Low, the 22.5 h.p. Sporting Model "Pick" is both fast and steady on the road.

No other modern sporting car is quite like the new 22.5 h.p. Pick, for it is a deliberate return to earlier types which had large slow speed engines. This car will give some of the pioneer motorists who are sometimes heard to argue a preference for the large engine as compared with the little high-speed motors of to-day, an opportunity to gratify their wishes at a very reasonable outlay. In its way the running of the Pick is unique ; the car is the modern equivalent of seven league boots, and covers the ground at a fine pace, with the engine ticking quietly round.

Judged in comparison with the majority of modern small car components, the gear box, like the engine, is of massive construction, having gears of ample size and large teeth. The gear change mechanism is operated through a side lever and gate and carried on a tunnel attached to the top of the box.

Now as to the running of the car. The engine develops 22 b.h.p. at 800 revolutions, and 43 at 2,000. The two-seater car complete weighs 22 cwt. Abnormally high gear ratios are fitted. The top gear is 2⅞, second 4¼, first 8½, and reverse 10 to 1. On top gear the engine turns over at roughly 1,000 revolutions per minute when the car is doing 40 m.p.h.

We have made a brief trial of the car and were impressed and intrigued by its speed performance. According to the reading of the speedometer, 60 m.p.h. is very easily reached, and at that speed the general quietness of running as compared with the usual type of sports car is truly remarkable ; there is no suggestion that the engine is really working hard. Despite the fact that an open exhaust pipe with no silencer was fitted, the exhaust noise is not at all pronounced to the occupants of the car, whilst at 40 m.p.h. the exhaust is practically inaudible, and the car ran in that comfortable style sometimes described as "going to sleep."

Because of the high gear ratios, the acceleration from comparatively slow speeds is not rapid, though at the upper end of the range it is decidedly better. The car holds the road very well ; the steering is good, and the springing comfortable.

The makers of the Pick Car are The Pick Motor Co., Stamford, and it should be recorded that they are amongst the pioneer manufacturers of this country, their experience dating back to belt-drive days.

Read copy of unsolicited letter to "Motor," October 16th.

High-reving v. Low-reving Engines.

" At the present time one hears so much about cars fitted with high efficiency high-revving engines, that I thought that my experience would perhaps be of interest to your readers. Within the past two years I have been running an 11.9 h.p. light car of high repute, also a 22.5 Pick car.

" The former is of the high-efficiency, high-revving type. The latter is of the low-speed type, and is fitted with abnormally high gears, its gear ratios being 2⅛ to 1 on top, 4½ to 1 on second speed, and 8½ to 1 on low.

" When I first took delivery of the Pick and was bringing it to Sunderland, during the first few miles, I thought that I was simply crawling, but when I reached Grantham (having come from Stamford, a distance of 22 miles) I looked at my watch and found that it had taken me exactly half an hour to do the 22 miles. I might add that I did not ' push ' the car at all. On reaching Sunderland I found that it had taken me five hours to do the distance of 190 miles.

" Now regarding the 11.9 h.p. light car : I have had a lot of trouble with it, the greatest being with the big-end bearings, also clutch and oil system, etc., etc. In fact, at the conclusion of 20,000 miles I find that I have nearly renewed the engine (reciprocating parts), also my engine was fitted with die-cast white-metal big-end bearings, which, as you know, are very hard, and I found, on taking the engine down, that the crankshaft was like a ploughed field—i.e., ridged.

" I know that there is no comparison between the horse-power of the two cars, but I reckon that what you spend in repairs of the smaller powered car easily outbalances the tax and repairs of the larger car per annum.

" Regarding speed, my 11.9 h.p. car is capable of 45 m.p.h. and the Pick will do 70 m.p.h. I have done 64 m.p.h. with four passengers, and have also had it up a hill of 1 in 3 gradient, which it climbed with ease. Petrol consumption of the two cars is as follows : 11.9 h.p. does 35 m.p.g., the Pick does 29¾ m.p.g. I know that Mr. Pick, the designer of the car, has absolutely gone against the present trend of automobile engine design, and I think that he is a very brave man to stick to the good old low-revving engine.

" I hope I shall see the day when we get the low-revving type back again, because there is too much wear and tear on the present-day engines.

" Stockton Road, Sunderland."

J. KISH.

Reprinted from "THE MOTOR," July 24th, 1923.

THE "SPORTS PICK" ON THE ROAD.

A Fast Car with Unusually High Gear Ratios.

The name of Pick takes one back to the old days of belt drive, when this make was of the single-lunger type, and it seems hardly possible that the present model can be the product of the same designer. Yet this is the case, and, what is more, certain features are even as unconventional as the old belt-drive car would be in this era.

Rated at 22.5 h.p., the new sporting model Pick is a return to the types that had big-capacity, low-speed power units, and even at 40 m.p.h. the revs. are only approximately 1,000 per minute. From this it will be gathered that even for the present-day super-efficient type of motor car the gearing is abnormally high—2⅛ to 1 on top, 4½ to 1 on second, 8½ to 1 on bottom, and 10 to 1 or. reverse! It is undoubtedly the highest-geared modern touring automobile produced to-day. Such, however, is the courage of the designer's convictions in his product, and we were indeed very sceptical on taking over the car for a run of 150 miles.

To one accustomed to handling the conventionally geared car, the Pick indeed comes as a novel and fascinating experience. It recalls the days of the old type Continental chain-driven productions, not in performance but in gearing. At 10-12 m.p.h. on top gear it is scarcely an exaggeration to say that one can count the beats of the engine, so slow does it turn over at this speed, and herein lies a marked feature of its fascination. At 30-40 m.p.h. it simply floats along,

and, despite the fact that a straight through exhaust was fitted, it is wonderfully quiet at this pace. Decelerating from the speed mentioned, the car still continues to float, and only a glance at the speedometer acquaints one with the fact that, with the foot off the accelerator, it is registering the limit laid down by law; but there it is, and it almost wants experiencing to believe it. Taking into consideration the gearing, the Pick has quite good acceleration, and 60 m.p.h. can very quickly be attained. Even then the engine does not rev. at more than 1,600 per minute.

The question, however, that we can hear being asked is, "Will it climb?" It apparently seems equal to all ordinary gradients on its 4½ to 1 second gear, for anything up to 40 m.p.h. is possible. Whether it will negotiate hills in the nature of a 1 in 5 gradient with ease is a point we were unable to prove, as our route did not lie over country of this nature. Gradients like Fitzjohn's Avenue and White Hill, on the main Henley-Maidenhead road, were taken at a very fast pace on second, and when in full swing any ordinary rise could be taken in its stride on top.

The suspension on the particular car we tried was open to some criticism on moderately rough roads, and there is no doubt that the addition of shock absorbers, which are contemplated as standard equipment, will very greatly improve the road-holding qualities and all-round comfort,

The Principle of the " PICK " Perfect Seat

(*Patent No. 20758.*)

The old method of seating.—The cushion is built up with vertical springs, the back being a fixture, when the seat is in use and the car gets a road shock, the passenger is bumped up and down, and a chafing is set up between the back of seat and the passenger, which is not correct.

In our method of seating, the back and bottom of seat work in conjunction, thus doing away with the chafing on the back of passenger, while the seats are sprung in such a way that they act as secondary road springs, which the ordinary seats fail to do.

Guarantee.

The following guarantee is given in lieu of any guarantee or Warranty either expressed or implied by Statute or otherwise; and is limited to a new car or chassis bought either direct from us, or from one of our duly authorised Agents, and no other guarantee or warranty whatever is given or is to be implied.

We guarantee that all precautions which are usual and reasonable have been taken to secure excellence of materials and workmanship in the chassis we sell. We, however, undertake to replace free of charge, within twelve months from date of delivery, any part or parts which, upon being returned to our works, carriage paid, we find to be defective in materials or workmanship.

This guarantee expressly excludes Cars which have been used for hire work, or cases where the defects have been caused by mis-use or neglect; and does not include any claims in respect of any articles such as Tyres, Electrical Goods or Accessories, which have not been manufactured by us.

THE PICK MOTOR CO., LTD., STAMFORD.

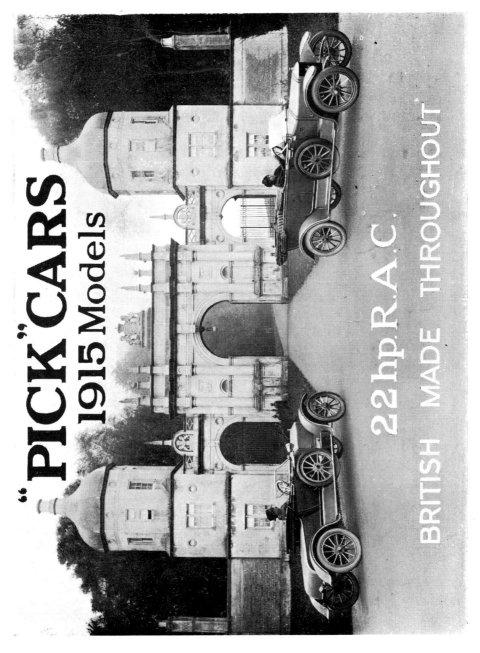

"PICK" CARS
1915 Models

22hp. R.A.C.

BRITISH MADE THROUGHOUT

"PICK" CARS AT BURGHLEY PARK.

Prospective purchasers are requested to view the lots before the Sale, as all lots will be sold from the Catalogue and not be visited during the time of sale.

Re The Pick Motor Co., Ltd., in Voluntary Liquidation.

THE PICK MOTOR WORKS
ST. MARTIN'S STAMFORD.

MESSRS. RICHARDSON

are instructed by Joseph Stephenson Esq., O.B.E., F.S.A.A., Liquidator and Receiver, to sell by Auction upon the above premises,

On Wednesday, January 21st, 1925
The whole of the valuable

Machinery and Stock-in-Trade

comprising :

Four Vertical Pillar Drilling Machines,
Three Bench Drilling Machines,
A Tool Grinder, A Gear Wheel Grinding Machine
A Spindle Keyway Cutting Machine,
A Facing and Boring Lathe, 14 Lathes, A Hardening Furnace
A 10 h.p. Electric Motor, A 5¼ h.p. ditto
A Portable Shop Crane, Two Forges,
An Acetylene Welding Set (new).

Three 22.5 h.p. Pick Motor Cars 1924 models
A 35 h.p. Pick Tractor, 5 Motor Bodies (unfinished)
The entire Stock of
Iron, Brass, Screws, Bolts, Nails, Paint, Tinman's Tools, Drills
A "Pratt" Petrol Pump and 500 gallon Tank
Office Furniture, The Garage Stock
and Miscellaneous Effects.

The Sale will commence at 10 o'clock.

Catalogues and further particulars may be obtained from the Auctioneers, Stamford and Bourne ; or Joseph Stephenson, Esq., O.B.E., F.S.A.A., Queen Street Chambers, Peterborough, and High Street, Stamford.

J. E. C. Potter, Printer, Stamford.

Plate 47: Title-page from the sales catalogue. *Stamford Museum*

128